The Constitution of
The State of Georgia:
A Quick Reference Guide

Bootblack Budget Books
Copyright 2018 ©
ISBN-13: 978-1985880245
ISBN-10: 1985880245

Contents:

Preamble – Page 26

Article I: Bill of Rights – Page 27

SECTION I: RIGHTS OF PERSONS

Paragraph I: Life, liberty, and property

Paragraph II: Protection to person and property; equal protection

Paragraph III: Freedom of conscience

Paragraph IV: Religious opinions; freedom of religion

Paragraph V: Freedom of speech and of the press guaranteed

Paragraph VI: Libel

Paragraph VII: Citizens, protection of

Paragraph VIII: Arms, right to keep and bear

Paragraph IX: Right to assemble and petition

Paragraph X: Bill of attainder; ex post facto laws; and retroactive laws

Paragraph XI: Right to trial by jury; number of jurors; selection and compensation of jurors

Paragraph XII: Right to the courts

Paragraph XIII: Searches, seizures, and warrants

Paragraph XIV: Benefit of counsel; accusation; list of witnesses; compulsory process

Paragraph XV: Habeas corpus

Paragraph XVI: Self-incrimination

Paragraph XVII: Bail; fines; punishment; arrest, abuse of prisoners

Paragraph XVIII: Jeopardy of life or liberty more than once forbidden

Paragraph XIX: Treason

Paragraph XX: Conviction, effect of

Paragraph XXI: Banishment and whipping as punishment for crime

Paragraph XXII: Involuntary servitude

Paragraph XXIII: Imprisonment for debt

Paragraph XXIV: Costs

Paragraph XXV: Status of the citizen

Paragraph XXVI: Exemptions from levy and sale

Paragraph XXVII: Spouse's separate property

Paragraph XXVIII: Enumeration of rights not denial of others

SECTION II: ORIGIN AND STRUCTURE OF GOVERNMENT

Paragraph I: Origin and foundation of government

Paragraph II: Object of government

Paragraph III: Separation of legislative, judicial, and executive powers

Paragraph IV: Contempts

Paragraph V: What acts void

Paragraph VI: Superiority of civil authority

Paragraph VII: Separation of church and state

Paragraph VIII: Lotteries and nonprofit bingo games

Paragraph IX: Sovereign immunity and waiver thereof; claims against the state and its departments, agencies, officers, and employees

SECTION III: GENERAL PROVISIONS

Paragraph I: Eminent domain.

Paragraph II: Private ways.

Paragraph III: Tidewater titles confirmed

Article II: Voting and Elections – Page 38

SECTION I: METHOD OF VOTING; RIGHT TO REGISTER AND VOTE

Paragraph I: Method of voting

Paragraph II: Right to register and vote

Paragraph III: Exceptions to right to register and vote

SECTION II: GENERAL PROVISIONS

Paragraph I: Procedures to be provided by law

Paragraph II: Run-off election

Paragraph III: Persons not eligible to hold office

Paragraph IV: Recall of public officials holding elective office

SECTION III: SUSPENSION AND REMOVAL OF PUBLIC OFFICIALS

Paragraph I: Procedures for and effect of suspending or removing public officials upon felony indictment

Paragraph II: Suspension upon felony conviction

Article III: Legislative Branch – Page 44

SECTION I: LEGISLATIVE POWER

Paragraph I: Power vested in General Assembly

SECTION II: COMPOSITION OF GENERAL ASSEMBLY

Paragraph I: Senate and House of Representatives

Paragraph II: Apportionment of General Assembly

Paragraph III: Qualifications of members of General Assembly

Paragraph IV: Disqualifications

SECTION III: OFFICERS OF THE GENERAL ASSEMBLY

Paragraph I: President and President Pro Tempore of the Senate

Paragraph II: Speaker and Speaker Pro Tempore of the House of Representatives

Paragraph III: Other officers of the two houses

SECTION IV: ORGANIZATION AND PROCEDURE OF THE GENERAL ASSEMBLY

Paragraph I: Meeting, time limit, and adjournment

Paragraph II: Oath of members

Paragraph III: Quorum

Paragraph IV: Rules of procedure; employees; interim committees

Paragraph V: Vacancies

Paragraph VI: Salaries

Paragraph VII: Election and returns; disorderly conduct

Paragraph VIII: Contempts, how punished

Paragraph IX: Privilege of members

Paragraph X: Elections by either house

Paragraph XI: Open meetings

SECTION V: ENACTMENT OF LAWS

Paragraph I: Journals and laws

Paragraph II: Bills for revenue

Paragraph III: One subject matter expressed

Paragraph IV: Statutes and sections of Code, how amended

Paragraph V: Majority of members to pass bill

Paragraph VI: When roll-call vote taken

Paragraph VII: Reading of general bills

Paragraph VIII: Procedure for considering local legislation

Paragraph IX: Advertisement of notice to introduce local legislation

Paragraph X: Acts signed

Paragraph XI: Signature of Governor

Paragraph XII: Rejected bills

Paragraph XIII: Approval, veto, and override of veto of bills and resolutions

Paragraph XIV: Jointly sponsored bills and resolutions

SECTION VI: EXERCISE OF POWER

Paragraph I: General powers

Paragraph II: Specific powers

Paragraph III: Powers not to be abridged

Paragraph IV: Limitations on special legislation

Paragraph V: Specific limitations

Paragraph VI: Gratuities

Paragraph VII: Regulation of alcoholic beverages

SECTION VII: IMPEACHMENTS

Paragraph I: Power to impeach

Paragraph II: Trial of impeachments

Paragraph III: Judgments in impeachment

SECTION VIII: INSURANCE REGULATION

Paragraph I: Regulation of insurance

Paragraph II: Issuance of licenses

SECTION IX: APPROPRIATIONS

Paragraph I: Public money, how drawn

Paragraph II: Preparation, submission, and enactments of general appropriations bill

Paragraph III: General appropriations bill

Paragraph IV: General appropriations Act

Paragraph V: Other or supplementary appropriations

Paragraph VI: Appropriations to be for specific sums

Paragraph VII: Appropriations void, when

SECTION X: RETIREMENT SYSTEMS

Paragraph I: Expenditure of public funds authorized

Paragraph II: Increasing benefits authorized

Paragraph III: Retirement systems covering employees of county boards of education

Paragraph IV: Firemen's Pension System

Paragraph V: Funding standards

Paragraph VA: Limitation on involuntary separation benefits for Governor of the State of Georgia

Paragraph VI: Involuntary separation; part-time service

Article IV: Constitutional Boards and Commissions – Page 73

SECTION I: PUBLIC SERVICE COMMISSION

Paragraph :. Public Service Commission

SECTION II: STATE BOARD OF PARDONS AND PAROLES

Paragraph I: State Board of Pardons and Paroles

Paragraph II: Powers and authority

SECTION III: STATE PERSONNEL BOARD

Paragraph I: State Personnel Board

Paragraph II: Veterans preference

SECTION IV: STATE TRANSPORTATION BOARD

Paragraph I: State Transportation Board; commissioner

SECTION V: VETERANS SERVICE BOARD

Paragraph I: Veterans Service Board; commissioner

SECTION VI: BOARD OF NATURAL RESOURCES

Paragraph I: Board of Natural Resources

SECTION VII: QUALIFICATIONS, COMPENSATION, REMOVAL FROM OFFICE, AND POWERS AND DUTIES OF MEMBERS OF CONSTITUTIONALBOARDS AND COMMISSIONS

Paragraph I: Qualifications, compensation, and removal from office

Paragraph II: Powers and duties

Article V: Executive Branch – Page 79

SECTION I: ELECTION OF GOVERNOR AND LIEUTENANT GOVERNOR

Paragraph I: Governor: term of office; compensation and allowances

Paragraph II: Election for Governor

Paragraph III: Lieutenant Governor

Paragraph IV: Qualifications of Governor and Lieutenant Governor

Paragraph V: Succession to executive power

Paragraph VI: Oath of office

SECTION II: DUTIES AND POWERS OF GOVERNOR

Paragraph I: Executive powers

Paragraph II: Law enforcement

Paragraph III: Commander in chief

Paragraph IV: Veto power

Paragraph V: Writs of election

Paragraph VI: Information and recommendations to the General Assembly

Paragraph VII: Special sessions of the General Assembly

Paragraph VIII: Filling vacancies

Paragraph IX. Appointments by Governor

Paragraph X. Information from officers and employees

SECTION III: OTHER ELECTED EXECUTIVE OFFICERS

Paragraph I: Other executive officers, how elected

Paragraph II: Qualifications

Paragraph III: Powers, duties, compensation, and allowances of other executive officers

Paragraph IV: Attorney General; duties

SECTION IV: DISABILITY OF EXECUTIVE OFFICERS

Paragraph I: "Elected constitutional executive officer," how defined

Paragraph II: Procedure for determining disability

Paragraph III: Effect of determination of disability

Article VI: Judicial Branch – Page 86

SECTION I: JUDICIAL POWER

Paragraph I: Judicial power of the state

Paragraph II: Unified judicial system:

Paragraph III: Judges; exercise of power outside own court; scope of term "judge:"

Paragraph IV: Exercise of judicial power

Paragraph V: Uniformity of jurisdiction, powers, etc:

Paragraph VI: Judicial circuits; courts in each county; court sessions

Paragraph VII: Judicial circuits, courts, and judgeships, law changed

Paragraph VIII: Transfer of cases

Paragraph IX: Rules of evidence; law prescribed

Paragraph X: Authorization for pilot projects

SECTION II: VENUE

Paragraph I: Divorce cases

Paragraph II: Land titles

Paragraph III: Equity cases

Paragraph IV: Suits against joint obligors, copartners, etc

Paragraph V: Suits against maker, endorser, etc

Paragraph VI: All other cases

Paragraph VII: Venue in third-party practice

Paragraph VIII: Power to change venue

SECTION III: CLASSES OF COURTS OF LIMITED JURISDICTION

Paragraph I: Jurisdiction of classes of courts of limited jurisdiction

SECTION IV: SUPERIOR COURTS

Paragraph I: Jurisdiction of superior courts

SECTION V: COURT OF APPEALS

Paragraph I: Composition of Court of Appeals; Chief Judge

Paragraph II: Panels as prescribed

Paragraph III: Jurisdiction of Court of Appeals; decisions binding

Paragraph IV: Certification of question to Supreme Court

Paragraph V: Equal division of court

SECTION VI: SUPREME COURT

Paragraph I: Composition of Supreme Court; Chief Justice; Presiding Justice; quorum; substitute judges

Paragraph II: Exclusive appellate jurisdiction of Supreme Court

Paragraph III: General appellate jurisdiction of Supreme Court

Paragraph IV: Jurisdiction over questions of law from state or federal appellate courts

Paragraph V: Review of cases in Court of Appeals

Paragraph VI: Decisions of Supreme Court binding

SECTION VII: SELECTION, TERM, COMPENSATION, AND DISCIPLINE OF JUDGES

Paragraph I: Election; term of office

Paragraph II: Qualifications

Paragraph III: Vacancies

Paragraph IV: Period of service of appointees

Paragraph V: Compensation and allowances of judges

Paragraph VI: Judicial Qualifications Commission; power; composition

Paragraph VII: Discipline, removal, and involuntary retirement of judges

Paragraph VIII: Due process; review by Supreme Court

SECTION VIII: DISTRICT ATTORNEYS

Paragraph I: District attorneys; vacancies; qualifications; compensation; duties; immunity

Paragraph II: Discipline, removal, and involuntary retirement of district attorneys

SECTION IX: GENERAL PROVISIONS

Paragraph I: Administration of the judicial system; uniform court rules; advice and consent of councils

Paragraph II: Disposition of cases

SECTION X: TRANSITION

Paragraph I: Effect of ratification: On the effective date of this article

Paragraph II: Continuation of judges

Article VII: Taxation and Finance – Page 100

SECTION I: POWER OF TAXATION

Paragraph I: Taxation; limitations on grants of tax powers

Paragraph II: Taxing power limited:

Paragraph III: Uniformity; classification of property; assessment of agricultural land; utilities

SECTION II: EXEMPTIONS FROM AD VALOREM TAXATION

Paragraph I: Unauthorized tax exemptions void

Paragraph II: Exemptions from taxation of property

Paragraph III: Exemptions which may be authorized locally

Paragraph IV: Current property tax exemptions preserved

Paragraph V: Disabled veteran's homestead exemption

SECTION III: PURPOSES AND METHOD OF STATE TAXATION

Paragraph I: Taxation; purposes for which powers may be exercised

Paragraph II: Revenue to be paid into general fund

Paragraph III: Grants to counties and municipalities

SECTION IV: STATE DEBT

Paragraph I: Purposes for which debt may be incurred

Paragraph II: State general obligation debt and guaranteed revenue debt; limitations

Paragraph III: State general obligation debt and guaranteed revenue debt; conditions upon issuance; sinking funds and reserve funds

Paragraph IV: Certain contracts prohibited

Paragraph V: Refunding of debt

Paragraph VI: Faith and credit of state pledged debt may be validated

Paragraph VII: Georgia State Financing and Investment Commission; duties

Paragraph VIII: State aid forbidden

Paragraph IX: Construction

Paragraph X: :Assumption of debts forbidden; exceptions

Paragraph XI: Section not to unlawfully impair contracts or revive obligations previously voided

Article VIII: Education – Page 122

SECTION I: PUBLIC EDUCATION

Paragraph I: Public education; free public education prior to college or postsecondary level; support by taxation

SECTION II: STATE BOARD OF EDUCATION

Paragraph I: State Board of Education

SECTION III: STATE SCHOOL SUPERINTENDENT

Paragraph I: State School Superintendent

SECTION IV: BOARD OF REGENTS

Paragraph I: University System of Georgia; board of regents

SECTION V: LOCAL SCHOOL SYSTEMS

Paragraph I: School systems continued; consolidation of school systems authorized; new independent school systems prohibited

Paragraph II: Boards of education

Paragraph III: School superintendents

Paragraph IV: Reserved

Paragraph V: Power of boards to contract with each other

Paragraph VI: Power of boards to accept bequests, donations, grants, and transfers

Paragraph VII: Special schools

SECTION VI: LOCAL TAXATION FOR EDUCATION

Paragraph I: Local taxation for education

Paragraph II: Increasing or removing tax rate

Paragraph III: School tax collection reimbursement

Paragraph IV: Sales tax for educational purposes

SECTION VII: EDUCATIONAL ASSISTANCE

Paragraph I: Educational assistance programs authorized

Paragraph II: Guaranteed revenue debt

Paragraph III: Public authorities

Paragraph IV: Waiver of tuition

Article XIX: Counties and Municipal Corporations – Page 134

SECTION I: COUNTIES

Paragraph I: Counties a body corporate and politic

Paragraph II: Number of counties limited; county boundaries and county sites; county consolidation

Paragraph III: County officers; election; term; compensation

Paragraph IV: Civil service systems

SECTION II: HOME RULE FOR COUNTIES AND MUNICIPALITIES

Paragraph I: Home rule for counties

Paragraph III: Supplementary powers

Paragraph IV: Planning and zoning

Paragraph V: Eminent domain

Paragraph VI: Special districts

Paragraph VII: Community redevelopment

Paragraph VIII: Limitation on the taxing power and contributions of counties, municipalities, and political subdivisions

Paragraph IX: Immunity of counties, municipalities, and school districts

SECTION III: INTERGOVERNMENTAL RELATIONS

Paragraph I: Intergovernmental contracts

Paragraph II: Local government reorganization

SECTION IV: TAXATION POWER OF COUNTY AND MUNICIPAL GOVERNMENTS

Paragraph I: Power of taxation

Paragraph II: Power of expenditure

Paragraph III: Purposes of taxation; allocation of taxes

Paragraph IV: Tax allocation; regional facilities

SECTION V: LIMITATION ON LOCAL DEBT

Paragraph I: Debt limitations of counties, municipalities, and other political subdivisions

Paragraph II: Special district debt

Paragraph III: Refunding of outstanding indebtedness

Paragraph IV: Exceptions to debt limitations

Paragraph V: Temporary loans authorized

Paragraph VI: Levy of taxes to pay bonds; sinking fund required

Paragraph VII: Validity of prior bond issues

SECTION VI: REVENUE BONDS

Paragraph I: Revenue bonds; general limitations

Paragraph II: Revenue bonds; special limitations

Paragraph III: Development authorities

Paragraph IV: Validation

Paragraph V: Validity of prior revenue bond issues

SECTION VII: COMMUNITY IMPROVEMENT DISTRICTS

Paragraph I: Creation

Paragraph II: Purposes

Paragraph III: Administration

Paragraph IV: Debt

Paragraph V: Cooperation with local governments

Paragraph VI: Regulation by general law

Article X: Amendments to the Constitution – Page 159

SECTION I: CONSTITUTION, HOW AMENDED

Paragraph I: Proposals to amend the Constitution; new Constitution

Paragraph II: Proposals by the General Assembly; submission to the people

Paragraph III: Repeal or amendment of proposal

Paragraph IV: Constitutional convention; how called

Paragraph V: Veto not permitted

Paragraph VI: Effective date of amendments or of a new Constitution

Article XI: Miscellaneous Provisions – Page 162

SECTION I: MISCELLANEOUS PROVISIONS

Paragraph I: Continuation of officers, boards, commissions, and authorities

Paragraph II: Preservation of existing laws; judicial review

Paragraph III: Proceedings of courts and administrative tribunals confirmed

Paragraph IV: Continuation of certain constitutional amendments for a period of four years

Paragraph V: Special commission created

Paragraph VI: Effective date

PREAMBLE

To perpetuate the principles of free government, insure justice to all, preserve peace, promote the interest and happiness of the citizen and of the family, and transmit to posterity the enjoyment of liberty, we the people of Georgia, relying upon the protection and guidance of Almighty God, do ordain and establish this Constitution.

ARTICLE I: BILL OF RIGHTS

SECTION I: RIGHTS OF PERSONS

Paragraph I. Life, liberty, and property
No person shall be deprived of life, liberty, or property except by due process of law.

Paragraph II. Protection to person and property; equal protection
Protection to person and property is the paramount duty of government and shall be impartial and complete. No person shall be denied the equal protection of the laws.
Paragraph III. Freedom of conscience. Each person has the natural and inalienable right to worship God, each according to the dictates of that person's own conscience; and no human authority should, in any case, control or interfere with such right of conscience.

Paragraph IV. Religious opinions; freedom of religion
No inhabitant of this state shall be molested in person or property or be prohibited from holding any public office or trust on account of religious opinions; but the right of freedom of religion shall not be so construed as to excuse acts of licentiousness or justify practices inconsistent with the peace and safety of the state.

Paragraph V. Freedom of speech and of the press guaranteed
No law shall be passed to curtail or restrain the freedom of speech or of the press. Every person may speak, write, and publish sentiments on all subjects but shall be responsible for the abuse of that liberty.

Paragraph VI. Libel
In all civil or criminal actions for libel, the truth may be given in evidence; and, if it shall appear to the trier of fact that the matter charged as libelous is true, the party shall be discharged.

Paragraph VII. Citizens, protection of
All citizens of the United States, resident in this state, are hereby declared citizens of this state; and it shall be the duty of the General Assembly to enact such laws as will protect them in the full enjoyment of the rights, privileges, and immunities due to such citizenship.

Paragraph VIII. Arms, right to keep and bear
The right of the people to keep and bear arms shall not be infringed, but the General Assembly shall have power to prescribe the manner in which arms may be borne.

Paragraph IX. Right to assemble and petition
The people have the right to assemble peaceably for their common good and to apply by petition or remonstrance to those vested with the powers of government for redress of grievances.
Paragraph X. Bill of attainder; ex post facto laws; and retroactive laws. No bill of attainder, ex post facto law, retroactive law, or laws impairing the obligation of contract or making irrevocable grant of special privileges or immunities shall be passed.
Paragraph XI. Right to trial by jury; number of jurors; selection and compensation of jurors.

(a) The right to trial by jury shall remain inviolate, except that the court shall render judgment without the verdict of a jury in all civil cases where no issuable defense is filed and where a jury is not demanded in writing by either party. In criminal cases, the defendant shall have a public and speedy trial by an impartial jury; and the jury shall be the judges of the law and the facts.
(b) A trial jury shall consist of 12 persons; but the General Assembly may prescribe any number, not less than six, to constitute a trial jury in courts of limited jurisdiction and in superior courts in misdemeanor cases.
(c) The General Assembly shall provide by law for the selection and compensation of persons to serve as grand jurors and trial jurors.

Paragraph XII. Right to the courts
No person shall be deprived of the right to prosecute or defend, either in person or by an attorney, that person's own cause in any of the courts of this state.

Paragraph XIII. Searches, seizures, and warrants
The right of the people to be secure in their persons, houses, papers, and effects against unreasonable searches and seizures shall not be violated; and no warrant shall issue except upon probable cause supported by oath or affirmation particularly describing the place or places to be searched and the persons or things to be seized.

Paragraph XIV. Benefit of counsel; accusation; list of witnesses; compulsory process
Every person charged with an offense against the laws of this state shall have the privilege and benefit of counsel; shall be furnished with a copy of the accusation or indictment and, on demand, with a list of the witnesses on whose testimony such charge is founded; shall have compulsory process to obtain the testimony of that person's own witnesses; and shall be confronted with the witnesses testifying against such person.
Paragraph XV. Habeas corpus. The writ of habeas corpus shall not be suspended unless, in case of rebellion or invasion, the public safety may require it.

Paragraph XVI. Self-incrimination
No person shall be compelled to give testimony tending in any manner to be self-incriminating.

Paragraph XVII. Bail; fines; punishment; arrest, abuse of prisoners.
Excessive bail shall not be required, nor excessive fines imposed, nor cruel and unusual punishments inflicted; nor shall any person be abused in being arrested, while under arrest, or in prison.

Paragraph XVIII. Jeopardy of life or liberty more than once forbidden

No person shall be put in jeopardy of life or liberty more than once for the same offense except when a new trial has been granted after conviction or in case of mistrial.

Paragraph XIX. Treason

Treason against the State of Georgia shall consist of insurrection against the state, adhering to the state's enemies, or giving them aid and comfort. No person shall be convicted of treason except on the testimony of two witnesses to the same overt act or confession in open court.

Paragraph XX. Conviction, effect of

No conviction shall work corruption of blood or forfeiture of estate.

Paragraph XXI. Banishment and whipping as punishment for crime

Neither banishment beyond the limits of the state nor whipping shall be allowed as a punishment for crime.

Paragraph XXII. Involuntary servitude. There shall be no involuntary servitude within the State of Georgia except as a punishment for crime after legal conviction thereof or for contempt of court.

Paragraph XXIII. Imprisonment for debt

There shall be no imprisonment for debt.

Paragraph XXIV. Costs

No person shall be compelled to pay costs in any criminal case except after conviction on final trial.

Paragraph XXV. Status of the citizen

The social status of a citizen shall never be the subject of legislation.

Paragraph XXVI. Exemptions from levy and sale
The General Assembly shall protect by law from levy and sale by virtue of any process under the laws of this state a portion of the property of each person in an amount of not less than $1,600.00 and shall have authority to define to whom any such additional exemptions shall be allowed; to specify the amount of such exemptions; to provide for the manner of exempting such property and for the sale, alienation, and encumbrance thereof; and to provide for the waiver of said exemptions by the debtor.
Paragraph XXVII. Spouse's separate property. The separate property of each spouse shall remain the separate property of that spouse except as otherwise provided by law.

Paragraph XXVIII. Fishing and hunting
The tradition of fishing and hunting and the taking of fish and wildlife shall be preserved for the people and shall be managed by law and regulation for the public good.

Paragraph XXIX. Enumeration of rights not denial of others
The enumeration of rights herein contained as a part of this Constitution shall not be construed to deny to the people any inherent rights which they may have hitherto enjoyed.

SECTION II. ORIGIN AND STRUCTURE OF GOVERNMENT

Paragraph I. Origin and foundation of government
All government, of right, originates with the people, is founded upon their will only, and is instituted solely for the good of the whole. Public officers are the trustees and servants of the people and are at all times amenable to them.

Paragraph II. Object of government
The people of this state have the inherent right of regulating their internal government. Government is instituted for the protection, security, and benefit of the people; and at all times they have the right to alter or reform the same whenever the public good may require it.

Paragraph III. Separation of legislative, judicial, and executive powers

The legislative, judicial, and executive powers shall forever remain separate and distinct; and no person discharging the duties of one shall at the same time exercise the functions of either of the others except as herein provided.

Paragraph IV. Contempts

The power of the courts to punish for contempt shall be limited by legislative acts.

Paragraph V. What acts void

Legislative acts in violation of this Constitution or the Constitution of the United States are void, and the judiciary shall so declare them.

Paragraph VI. Superiority of civil authority

The civil authority shall be superior to the military.

Paragraph VII. Separation of church and state

No money shall ever be taken from the public treasury, directly or indirectly, in aid of any church, sect, cult, or religious denomination or of any sectarian institution.

Paragraph VIII. Lotteries and nonprofit bingo games

(a) Except as herein specifically provided in this Paragraph VIII, all lotteries, and the sale of lottery tickets, and all forms of pari-mutuel betting and casino gambling are hereby prohibited; and this prohibition shall be enforced by penal laws.
(b) The General Assembly may by law provide that the operation of a nonprofit bingo game shall not be a lottery and shall be legal in this state. The General Assembly may by law define a nonprofit bingo game and provide for the regulation of nonprofit bingo games.
(c) The General Assembly may by law provide for the operation and regulation of a lottery or lotteries by or on behalf of the state and for any matters relating to the purposes or provisions of this

subparagraph. Proceeds derived from the lottery or lotteries operated by or on behalf of the state shall be used to pay the operating expenses of the lottery or lotteries, including all prizes, without any appropriation required by law, and for educational programs and purposes as hereinafter provided. Lottery proceeds shall not be subject to Article VII, Section III, Paragraph II; Article III, Section IX, Paragraph VI(a); or Article III, Section IX, Paragraph IV(c), except that the net proceeds after payment of such operating expenses shall be subject to Article VII, Section III, Paragraph II. Net proceeds after payment of such operating expenses shall be separately accounted for and shall be specifically identified by the Governor in his annual budget presented to the General Assembly as a separate budget category entitled 'Lottery Proceeds' and the Governor shall make specific recommendations as to educational programs and educational purposes to which said net proceeds shall be appropriated. In the General Appropriations Act adopted by the General Assembly, the General Assembly shall appropriate all net proceeds of the lottery or lotteries by such separate budget category to educational programs and educational purposes. Such net proceeds shall be used to support improvements and enhancements for educational programs and purposes and such net proceeds shall be used to supplement, not supplant, non-lottery educational resources for educational programs and purposes. The educational programs and educational purposes for which proceeds may be so appropriated shall include only the following:

(1) Tuition grants, scholarships, or loans to citizens of this state to enable such citizens to attend colleges and universities located within this state, regardless of whether such colleges or universities are operated by the board of regents, or to attend institutions operated under the authority of the Department of Technical and Adult Education;
(2) Voluntary pre-kindergarten;
(3) One or more educational shortfall reserves in a total amount of not less than 10 percent of the net proceeds of the lottery for the preceding fiscal year;

(4) Costs of providing to teachers at accredited public institutions who teach levels K-12, personnel at public postsecondary technical institutes under the authority of the Department of Technical and Adult Education, and professors and instructors within the University System of Georgia the necessary training in the use and application of computers and advanced electronic instructional technology to implement interactive learning environments in the classroom and to access the state-wide distance learning network; and
(5) Capital outlay projects for educational facilities; provided, however, that no funds shall be appropriated for the items listed in paragraphs (4) and (5) of this subsection until all persons eligible for and applying for assistance as provided in paragraph **(1)** of this subsection have received such assistance, all approved pre-kindergarten programs provided for in paragraph **(2)** of this subsection have been fully funded, and the education shortfall reserve or reserves provided for in paragraph **(3)** of this subsection have been fully funded.

(d) On and after January 1, 1995, the holding of raffles by nonprofit organizations shall be lawful and shall not be prohibited by any law enacted prior to January 1, 1994. Laws enacted on or after January 1, 1994, however, may restrict, regulate, or prohibit the operation of such raffles.

Paragraph IX. Sovereign immunity and waiver thereof; claims against the state and its departments, agencies, officers, and employees

(a) The General Assembly may waive the state's sovereign immunity from suit by enacting a State Tort Claims Act, in which the General Assembly may provide by law for procedures for the making, handling, and disposition of actions or claims against the state and its departments, agencies, officers, and employees, upon such terms and subject to such conditions and limitations as the General Assembly may provide.

(b) The General Assembly may also provide by law for the processing and disposition of claims against the state which do not exceed such maximum amount as provided therein.
(c) The state's defense of sovereign immunity is hereby waived as to any action ex contractu for the breach of any written contract now existing or hereafter entered into by the state or its departments and agencies.
(d) Except as specifically provided by the General Assembly in a State Tort Claims Act, all officers and employees of the state or its departments and agencies may be subject to suit and may be liable for injuries and damages caused by the negligent performance of, or negligent failure to perform, their ministerial functions and may be liable for injuries and damages if they act with actual malice or with actual intent to cause injury in the performance of their official functions. Except as provided in this subparagraph, officers and employees of the state or its departments and agencies shall not be subject to suit or liability, and no judgment shall be entered against them, for the performance or nonperformance of their official functions. The provisions of this subparagraph shall not be waived.
(e) Except as specifically provided in this Paragraph, sovereign immunity extends to the state and all of its departments and agencies. The sovereign immunity of the state and its departments and agencies can only be waived by an Act of the General Assembly which specifically provides that sovereign immunity is thereby waived and the extent of such waiver. (f) No waiver of sovereign immunity under this Paragraph shall be construed as a waiver of any immunity provided to the state or its departments, agencies, officers, or employees by the United States Constitution.

SECTION III. GENERAL PROVISIONS

Paragraph I. Eminent domain

(a) Except as otherwise provided in this Paragraph, private property shall not be taken or damaged for public purposes without just and adequate compensation being first paid.

(b) When private property is taken or damaged by the state or the counties or municipalities of the state for public road or street purposes, or for public transportation purposes, or for any other public purposes as determined by the General Assembly, just and adequate compensation therefor need not be paid until the same has been finally fixed and determined as provided by law; but such just and adequate compensation shall then be paid in preference to all other obligations except bonded indebtedness.
(c) The General Assembly may by law require the condemnor to make prepayment against adequate compensation as a condition precedent to the exercise of the right of eminent domain and provide for the disbursement of the same to the end that the rights and equities of the property owner, lien holders, and the state and its subdivisions may be protected.
(d) The General Assembly may provide by law for the payment by the condemnor of reasonable expenses, including attorney's fees, incurred by the condemnee in determining just and adequate compensation.
(e) Notwithstanding any other provision of the Constitution, the General Assembly may provide by law for relocation assistance and payments to persons displaced through the exercise of the power of eminent domain or because of public projects or programs; and the powers of taxation may be exercised and public funds expended in furtherance thereof.

Paragraph II. Private ways
In case of necessity, private ways may be granted upon just and adequate compensation being first paid by the applicant.

Paragraph III. Tidewater titles confirmed
The Act of the General Assembly approved December 16, 1902, which extends the title of ownership of lands abutting on tidal water to low water mark, is hereby ratified and confirmed.

SECTION IV. MARRIAGE

Paragraph I. Recognition of marriage

(a) This state shall recognize as marriage only the union of man and woman. Marriages between persons of the same sex are prohibited in this state.
(b) No union between persons of the same sex shall be recognized by this state as entitled to the benefits of marriage. This state shall not give effect to any public act, record, or judicial proceeding of any other state or jurisdiction respecting a relationship between persons of the same sex that is treated as a marriage under the laws of such other state or jurisdiction. The courts of this state shall have no jurisdiction to grant a divorce or separate maintenance with respect to any such relationship or otherwise to consider or rule on any of the parties' respective rights arising as a result of or in connection with such relationship.

ARTICLE II: VOTING AND ELECTIONS

SECTION I. METHOD OF VOTING; RIGHT TO REGISTER AND VOTE

Paragraph I. Method of voting
Elections by the people shall be by secret ballot and shall be conducted in accordance with procedures provided by law.

Paragraph II. Right to register and vote
Every person who is a citizen of the United States and a resident of Georgia as defined by law, who is at least 18 years of age and not disenfranchised by this article, and who meets minimum residency requirements as provided by law shall be entitled to vote at any election by the people. The General Assembly shall provide by law for the registration of electors.

Paragraph III. Exceptions to right to register and vote

(a) No person who has been convicted of a felony involving moral turpitude may register, remain registered, or vote except upon completion of the sentence.

(b) No person who has been judicially determined to be mentally incompetent may register, remain registered, or vote unless the disability has been removed.

SECTION II. GENERAL PROVISIONS

Paragraph I. Procedures to be provided by law
The General Assembly shall provide by law for a method of appeal from the decision to allow or refuse to allow any person to register or vote and shall provide by law for a procedure whereby returns of all elections by the people shall be made to the Secretary of State.

Paragraph II. Run-off election
A run-off election shall be a continuation of the general election and only persons who were entitled to vote in the general election shall be entitled to vote therein; and only those votes cast for the persons designated for the runoff shall be counted in the tabulation and canvass of the votes cast.

Paragraph III. Persons not eligible to hold office
No person who is not a registered voter; who has been convicted of a felony involving moral turpitude, unless that person's civil rights have been restored and at least ten years have elapsed from the date of the completion of the sentence without a subsequent conviction of another felony involving moral turpitude; who is a defaulter for any federal, state, county, municipal, or school system taxes required of such officeholder or candidate if such person has been finally adjudicated by a court of competent jurisdiction to owe those taxes, but such ineligibility may be removed at any time by full payment thereof, or by making payments to the tax authority pursuant to a payment plan, or under such other conditions as the General Assembly may provide by general law; or who is the holder of public funds illegally shall be eligible to hold any office or appointment of honor or trust in this state. Additional conditions of eligibility to hold office for persons elected on a write-in vote and for persons holding offices or appointments of honor or trust other than elected offices created by this Constitution may be provided by law.

Paragraph IV. Recall of public officials holding elective office
The General Assembly is hereby authorized to provide by general law for the recall of public officials who hold elective office. The procedures, grounds, and all other matters relative to such recall shall be provided for in such law.

Paragraph V. Vacancies created by elected officials qualifying for other office

The office of any state, county, or municipal elected official shall be declared vacant upon such elected official qualifying, in a general primary or general election, or special primary or special election, for another state, county, or municipal elective office or qualifying for the House of Representatives or the Senate of the United States if the term of the office for which such official is qualifying for begins more than 30 days prior to the expiration of such official's present term of office. The vacancy created in any such office shall be filled as provided by this Constitution or any general or local law. This provision shall not apply to any elected official seeking or holding more than one elective office when the holding of such offices simultaneously is specifically authorized by law.

SECTION III. SUSPENSION AND REMOVAL OF PUBLIC OFFICIALS

Paragraph I. Procedures for and effect of suspending or removing public officials upon felony indictment

(a) As used in this Paragraph, the term 'public official' means the Governor, the Lieutenant Governor, the Secretary of State, the Attorney General, the State School Superintendent, the Commissioner of Insurance, the Commissioner of Agriculture, the Commissioner of Labor, and any member of the General Assembly.

(b) Upon indictment for a felony by a grand jury of this state or by the United States, which felony indictment relates to the performance or activities of the office of any public official, the Attorney General or district attorney shall transmit a certified copy of the indictment to the Governor or, if the indicted public official is the Governor, to the Lieutenant Governor who shall, subject to subparagraph (d) of this Paragraph, appoint a review commission. If the indicted public official is the Governor, the commission shall be composed of the Attorney General, the Secretary of State, the State School Superintendent, the

Commissioner of Insurance, the Commissioner of Agriculture, and the Commissioner of Labor. If the indicted public official is the Attorney General, the commission shall be composed of three other public officials who are not members of the General Assembly. If the indicted public official is not the Governor, the Attorney General, or a member of the General Assembly, the commission shall be composed of the Attorney General and two other public officials who are not members of the General Assembly. If the indicted public official is a member of the General Assembly, the commission shall be composed of the Attorney General and one member of the Senate and one member of the House of Representatives. If the Attorney General brings the indictment against the public official, the Attorney General shall not serve on the commission. In place of the Attorney General, the Governor shall appoint a retired Supreme Court Justice or a retired Court of Appeals Judge. The commission shall provide for a speedy hearing, including notice of the nature and cause of the hearing, process for obtaining witnesses, and the assistance of counsel. Unless a longer period of time is granted by the appointing authority, the commission shall make a written report within 14 days. If the commission determines that the indictment relates to and adversely affects the administration of the office of the indicted public official and that the rights and interests of the public are adversely affected thereby, the Governor or, if the Governor is the indicted public official, the Lieutenant Governor shall suspend the public official immediately and without further action pending the final disposition of the case or until the expiration of the officer's term of office, whichever occurs first. During the term of office to which such officer was elected and in which the indictment occurred, if a nolle prosequi is entered, if the public official is acquitted, or if after conviction the conviction is later overturned as a result of any direct appeal or application for a writ of certiorari, the officer shall be immediately reinstated to the office from which he was suspended. While a public official is suspended under this Paragraph and until initial conviction by the trial court, the officer shall continue to receive the compensation from his office. After initial conviction by the trial court, the officer shall not be entitled to receive the compensation from his office. If the officer is reinstated to office, he shall be entitled to receive any compensation withheld under the provisions of this Paragraph.

(c) Unless the Governor is the public officer under suspension, for the duration of any suspension under this Paragraph, the Governor shall appoint a replacement officer except in the case of a member of the General Assembly. If the Governor is the public officer under suspension, the provisions of Article V, Section I, Paragraph V of this Constitution shall apply as if the Governor were temporarily disabled. Upon a final conviction with no appeal or review pending, the office shall be declared vacant and a successor to that office shall be chosen as provided in this Constitution or the laws enacted in pursuance thereof.

(d) No commission shall be appointed for a period of 14 days from the day the indictment is received. This period of time may be extended by the Governor. During this period of time, the indicted public official may, in writing, authorize the Governor or, if the Governor is the indicted public official, the Lieutenant Governor to suspend him from office. Any such voluntary suspension shall be subject to the same conditions for review, reinstatement, or declaration of vacancy as are provided in this Paragraph for a nonvoluntary suspension.

(e) After any suspension is imposed under this Paragraph, the suspended public official may petition the appointing authority for a review. The Governor or, if the indicted public official is the Governor, the Lieutenant Governor may reappoint the commission to review the suspension. The commission shall make a written report within 14 days. If the commission recommends that the public official be reinstated, he shall immediately be reinstated to office.

(f) The report and records of the commission and the fact that the public official has or has not been suspended shall not be admissible in evidence in any court for any purpose. The report and record of the commission shall not be open to the public.

(g) The provisions of this Paragraph shall not apply to any indictment handed down prior to January 1, 1985.

(h) If a public official who is suspended from office under the provisions of this Paragraph is not first tried at the next regular or special term following the indictment, the suspension shall be terminated and the public official shall be reinstated to office. The public official shall not be reinstated under this subparagraph if he is not so tried based on a continuance granted upon a motion made only by the defendant.

Paragraph II. Suspension upon felony conviction
Upon initial conviction of any public official designated in Paragraph I of this section for any felony in a trial court of this state or the United States, regardless of whether the officer has been suspended previously under Paragraph I of this section, such public official shall be immediately and without further action suspended from office. While a public official is suspended from office under this Paragraph, he or she shall not be entitled to receive the compensation from his or her office. If, during the remainder of the elected official's term of office, the conviction is later overturned as a result of any direct appeal or application for a writ of certiorari, the public official shall be immediately reinstated to the office from which he or she was suspended and shall be entitled to receive any compensation withheld under the provisions of this Paragraph. Unless the Governor is the public official under suspension, for the duration of any suspension under this Paragraph, the Governor shall appoint a replacement official except in the case of a member of the General Assembly. If the public officer under suspension is a member of the Senate or House of Representatives, then a replacement member for the duration of the suspension shall be elected as now or hereafter provided by law, in a manner the same as or similar to the election of a member to fill a vacancy in the General Assembly but to serve only for the duration of the suspension. If the Governor is the public officer under suspension, the provisions of Article V, Section I, Paragraph V of this Constitution shall apply as if the Governor were temporarily disabled. Upon a final conviction with no appeal or review pending, the office shall be declared vacant and a successor to that office shall be chosen as provided in this Constitution or the laws enacted in pursuance thereof. The provisions of this Paragraph shall not apply to any conviction rendered prior to January 1, 1987.

ARTICLE III: LEGISLATIVE BRANCH

SECTION I. LEGISLATIVE POWER

Paragraph I. Power vested in General Assembly
The legislative power of the state shall be vested in a General Assembly which shall consist of a Senate and a House of Representatives.

SECTION II. COMPOSITION OF GENERAL ASSEMBLY

Paragraph I. Senate and House of Representatives

(a) The Senate shall consist of not more than 56 Senators, each of whom shall be elected from single-member districts.
(b) The House of Representatives shall consist of not fewer than 180 Representatives apportioned among representative districts of the state.

Paragraph II. Apportionment of General Assembly
The General Assembly shall apportion the Senate and House districts. Such districts shall be composed of contiguous territory. The apportionment of the Senate and of the House of Representatives shall be changed by the General Assembly as necessary after each United States decennial census.

Paragraph III. Qualifications of members of General Assembly

(a) At the time of their election, the members of the Senate shall be citizens of the United States, shall be at least 25 years of age, shall have been citizens of this state for at least two years, and shall have been legal residents of the territory embraced within the district from which elected for at least one year.
(b) At the time of their election, the members of the House of Representatives shall be citizens of the United States, shall be at least 21 years of age, shall have been citizens of this state for at least two years, and shall have been legal residents of the

territory embraced within the district from which elected for at least one year.

Paragraph IV. Disqualifications

(a) No person on active duty with any branch of the armed forces of the United States shall have a seat in either house unless otherwise provided by law.
(b) No person holding any civil appointment or office having any emolument annexed thereto under the United States, this state, or any other state shall have a seat in either house.
(c) No Senator or Representative shall be elected by the General Assembly or appointed by the Governor to any office or appointment having any emolument annexed thereto during the time for which such person shall have been elected unless the Senator or Representative shall first resign the seat to which elected; provided, however, that, during the term for which elected, no Senator or Representative shall be appointed to any civil office which has been created during such term.

Paragraph V. Election and term of members

(a) The members of the General Assembly shall be elected by the qualified electors of their respective districts for a term of two years and shall serve until the time fixed for the convening of the next General Assembly.
(b) The members of the General Assembly in office on June 30, 1983, shall serve out the remainder of the terms to which elected.
(c) The first election for members of the General Assembly under this Constitution shall take place on Tuesday after the first Monday in November, 1984, and subsequent elections biennially on that day until the day of election is changed by law.

SECTION III. OFFICERS OF THE GENERAL ASSEMBLY

Paragraph I. President and President Pro Tempore of the Senate

(a) The presiding officer of the Senate shall be styled the President of the Senate.
(b) A President Pro Tempore shall be elected by the Senate from among its members. The President Pro Tempore shall act as President in case of the temporary disability of the President. In case of the death, resignation, or permanent disability of the President or in the event of the succession of the President to the executive power, the President Pro Tempore shall become President and shall receive the same compensation and allowances as the Speaker of the House of Representatives. The General Assembly shall provide by law for the method of determining disability as provided in this Paragraph.

Paragraph II. Speaker and Speaker Pro Tempore of the House of Representatives

(a) The presiding officer of the House of Representatives shall be styled the Speaker of the House of Representatives and shall be elected by the House of Representatives from among its members.
(b) A Speaker Pro Tempore shall be elected by the House of Representatives from among its members. The Speaker Pro Tempore shall become Speaker in case of the death, resignation, or permanent disability of the Speaker and shall serve until a Speaker is elected. Such election shall be held as provided in the rules of the House. The General Assembly shall provide by law for the method of determining disability as provided in this Paragraph.

Paragraph III. Other officers of the two houses
The other officers of the two houses shall be a Secretary of the Senate and a Clerk of the House of Representatives.

SECTION IV. ORGANIZATION AND PROCEDURE OF THE GENERAL ASSEMBLY

Paragraph I. Meeting, time limit, and adjournment\

(a) The Senate and House of Representatives shall organize each odd-numbered year and shall be a different General Assembly for each two-year period. The General Assembly shall meet in regular session on the second Monday in January of each year, or otherwise as provided by law, and may continue in session for a period of no longer than 40 days in the aggregate each year. By concurrent resolution, the General Assembly may adjourn any regular session to such later date as it may fix for reconvening. Separate periods of adjournment may be fixed by one or more such concurrent resolutions.
(b) Neither house shall adjourn during a regular session for more than three days or meet in any place other than the state capitol without the consent of the other. Following the fifth day of a special session, either house may adjourn not more than twice for a period not to exceed seven days for each such adjournment. In the event either house, after the thirtieth day of any session, adopts a resolution to adjourn for a specified period of time and such resolution and any amendments thereto are not adopted by both houses by the end of the legislative day on which adjournment was called for in such resolution, the Governor may adjourn both houses for a period of time not to exceed ten days.
(c) If an impeachment trial is pending at the end of any session, the House shall adjourn and the Senate shall remain in session until such trial is completed.

Paragraph II. Oath of members
Each Senator and Representative, before taking the seat to which elected, shall take the oath or affirmation prescribed by law.

Paragraph III. Quorum
A majority of the members to which each house is entitled shall constitute a quorum to transact business. A smaller number may adjourn from day to day and compel the presence of its absent members.

Paragraph IV. Rules of procedure; employees; interim committees
Each house shall determine its rules of procedure and may provide for its employees. Interim committees may be created by or pursuant to the authority of the General Assembly or of either house.

Paragraph V. Vacancies
When a vacancy occurs in the General Assembly, it shall be filled as provided by this Constitution and by law. The seat of a member of either house shall be vacant upon the removal of such member's legal residence from the district from which elected.

Paragraph VI. Salaries
The members of the General Assembly shall receive such salary as shall be provided for by law, provided that no increase in salary shall become effective prior to the end of the term during which such change is made.

Paragraph VII. Election and returns; disorderly conduct.
Each house shall be the judge of the election, returns, and qualifications of its members and shall have power to punish them for disorderly behavior or misconduct by censure, fine, imprisonment, or expulsion; but no member shall be expelled except by a vote of two-thirds of the members of the house to which such member belongs.

Paragraph VIII. Contempts, how punished
Each house may punish by imprisonment, not extending beyond the session, any person not a member who shall be guilty of a contempt by any disorderly behavior in its presence or who shall rescue or attempt to rescue any person arrested by order of either house.

Paragraph IX. Privilege of members
The members of both houses shall be free from arrest during sessions of the General Assembly, or committee meetings thereof, and in going thereto or returning therefrom, except for treason, felony, or breach of the peace. No member shall be liable to answer in any other place for anything spoken in either house or in any committee meeting of either house.

Paragraph X. Elections by either house
All elections by either house of the General Assembly shall be by recorded vote, and the vote shall appear on the respective journal of each house.

Paragraph XI. Open meetings
The sessions of the General Assembly and all standing committee meetings thereof shall be open to the public. Either house may by rule provide for exceptions to this requirement.

SECTION V. ENACTMENT OF LAWS

Paragraph I. Journals and laws
Each house shall keep and publish after its adjournment a journal of its proceedings. The original journals shall be the sole, official records of the proceedings of each house and shall be preserved as provided by law. The General Assembly shall provide for the publication of the laws passed at each session.

Paragraph II. Bills for revenue
All bills for raising revenue, or appropriating money, shall originate in the House of Representatives.

Paragraph III. One subject matter expressed
No bill shall pass which refers to more than one subject matter or contains matter different from what is expressed in the title thereof.

Paragraph IV. Statutes and sections of Code, how amended
No law or section of the Code shall be amended or repealed by mere reference to its title or to the number of the section of the Code; but the amending or repealing Act shall distinctly describe the law or Code section to be amended or repealed as well as the alteration to be made.

Paragraph V. Majority of members to pass bill
No bill shall become law unless it shall receive a majority of the votes of all the members to which each house is entitled, and such vote shall so appear on the journal of each house.

Paragraph VI. When roll-call vote taken
In either house, when ordered by the presiding officer or at the desire of one-fifth of the members present or a lesser number if so provided by the rules of either house, a roll-call vote on any question shall be taken and shall be entered on the journal. The yeas and nays in each house shall be recorded and entered on the journal upon the passage or rejection of any bill or resolution appropriating money and whenever the Constitution requires a vote of two-thirds of either or both houses for the passage of a bill or resolution.

Paragraph VII. Reading of general bills
The title of every general bill and of every resolution intended to have the effect of general law or to amend this Constitution or to propose a new Constitution shall be read three times and on three separate days in each house before such bill or resolution shall be voted upon; and the third reading of such bill and resolution shall be in their entirety when ordered by the presiding officer or by a majority of the members voting on such question in either house.

Paragraph VIII. Procedure for considering local legislation

The General Assembly may provide by law for the procedure for considering local legislation. The title of every local bill and every resolution intended to have the effect of local law shall be read at least once before such bill or resolution shall be voted upon; and no such bill or resolution shall be voted upon prior to the second day following the day of introduction.

Paragraph IX. Advertisement of notice to introduce local legislation

The General Assembly shall provide by law for the advertisement of notice of intention to introduce local bills.

Paragraph X. Acts signed

All Acts shall be signed by the President of the Senate and the Speaker of the House of Representatives.

Paragraph XI. Signature of Governor

No provision in this Constitution for a two-thirds' vote of both houses of the General Assembly shall be construed to waive the necessity for the signature of the Governor as in any other case, except in the case of the two-thirds' vote required to override the veto or to submit proposed constitutional amendments or a proposal for a new Constitution.

Paragraph XII. Rejected bills

No bill or resolution intended to have the effect of law which shall have been rejected by either house shall again be proposed during the same regular or special session under the same or any other title without the consent of two-thirds of the house by which the same was rejected.

Paragraph XIII. Approval, veto, and override of veto of bills and resolutions

(a) All bills and all resolutions which have been passed by the General Assembly intended to have the effect of law shall become law if the Governor approves or fails to veto the same within six days from the date any such bill or resolution is transmitted to the Governor unless the General Assembly adjourns sine die or adjourns for more than 40 days prior to the expiration of said six days. In the case of such adjournment sine die or of such adjournment for more than 40 days, the same shall become law if approved or not vetoed by the Governor within 40 days from the date of any such adjournment.

(b) During sessions of the General Assembly or during any period of adjournment of a session of the General Assembly, no bill or resolution shall be transmitted to the Governor after passage except upon request of the Governor or upon order of two-thirds of the membership of each house. A local bill which is required by the Constitution to have a referendum election conducted before it shall become effective shall be transmitted immediately to the Governor when ordered by the presiding officer of the house wherein the bill shall have originated or upon order of two-thirds of the membership of such house.

(c) The Governor shall have the duty to transmit any vetoed bill or resolution, together with the reasons for such veto, to the presiding officer of the house wherein it originated within three days from the date of veto if the General Assembly is in session on the date of transmission. If the General Assembly adjourns sine die or adjourns for more than 40 days, the Governor shall transmit any vetoed bill or resolution, together with the reasons for such veto, to the presiding officer of the house wherein it originated within 60 days of the date of such adjournment.

(d) During sessions of the General Assembly, any vetoed bill or resolution may upon receipt be immediately considered by the house wherein it originated for the purpose of overriding the veto. If two-thirds of the members to which such house is entitled vote to override the veto of the Governor, the same shall be immediately transmitted to the other house where it shall be

immediately considered. Upon the vote to override the veto by two-thirds of the members to which such other house is entitled, such bill or resolution shall become law. All bills and resolutions vetoed during the last three days of the session and not considered for the purpose of overriding the veto and all bills and resolutions vetoed after the General Assembly has adjourned sine die may be considered at the next session of the General Assembly for the purpose of overriding the veto in the manner herein provided. If either house shall fail to override the Governor's veto, neither house shall again consider such bill or resolution for the purpose of overriding such veto.
(e) The Governor may approve any appropriation and veto any other appropriation in the same bill, and any appropriation vetoed shall not become law unless such veto is overridden in the manner herein provided.

Paragraph XIV. Jointly sponsored bills and resolutions
The General Assembly may provide by law for the joint sponsorship of bills and resolutions.

SECTION VI. EXERCISE OF POWERS

Paragraph I. General powers
The General Assembly shall have the power to make all laws not inconsistent with this Constitution, and not repugnant to the Constitution of the United States, which it shall deem necessary and proper for the welfare of the state.

Paragraph II. Specific powers

(a) Without limitation of the powers granted under Paragraph I, the General Assembly shall have the power to provide by law for:
(1) Restrictions upon land use in order to protect and preserve the natural resources, environment, and vital areas of this state.
(2) A militia and for the trial by courts-martial and nonjudicial punishment of its members, the discipline of whom, when not in federal service, shall be in accordance with law and the directives of the Governor acting as commander in chief.

(3) The participation by the state and political subdivisions and instrumentalities of the state in federal programs and the compliance with laws relating thereto, including but not limited to the powers, which may be exercised to the extent and in the manner necessary to effect such participation and compliance, to tax, to expend public money, to condemn property, and to zone property.

(4) The continuity of state and local governments in periods of emergency resulting from disasters caused by enemy attack including but not limited to the suspension of all constitutional legislative rules during such emergency.

(5) The participation by the state with any county, municipality, nonprofit organization, or any combination thereof in the operation of any of the facilities operated by such agencies for the purpose of encouraging and promoting tourism in this state.

(6) The control and regulation of outdoor advertising devices adjacent to federal aid interstate and primary highways and for the acquisition of property or interest therein for such purposes and may exercise the powers of taxation and provide for the expenditure of public funds in connection therewith.

(b) The General Assembly shall have the power to implement the provisions of Article I, Section III, Paragraph I(2.); Article IV, Section VIII, Paragraph II; Article IV, Section VIII, Paragraph III; and Article X, Section II, Paragraph XII of the Constitution of 1976 in force and effect on June 30, 1983; and all laws heretofore adopted thereunder and valid at the time of their enactment shall continue in force and effect until modified or repealed.

(c) The distribution of tractors, farm equipment, heavy equipment, new motor vehicles, and parts therefor in the State of Georgia vitally affects the general economy of the state and the public interest and public welfare. Notwithstanding the provisions of Article I, Section I, Paragraphs I, II, and III or Article III, Section VI, Paragraph V(c) of this Constitution, the General Assembly in the exercise of its police power shall be authorized to regulate tractor, farm equipment, heavy equipment, and new motor vehicle manufacturers, distributors, dealers, and their representatives doing business in Georgia, including agreements among such parties, in order to prevent frauds, unfair business practices, unfair methods of competition, impositions, and other abuses upon its citizens. Any law enacted by the General Assembly shall not impair the obligation of an existing contract but may apply with respect to the renewal of such a contract after the effective date of such law.

Paragraph III. Powers not to be abridged
The General Assembly shall not abridge its powers under this Constitution. No law enacted by the General Assembly shall be construed to limit its powers.

Paragraph IV. Limitations on special legislation

(a) Laws of a general nature shall have uniform operation throughout this state and no local or special law shall be enacted in any case for which provision has been made by an existing general law, except that the General Assembly may by general law authorize local governments by local ordinance or resolution to exercise police powers which do not conflict with general laws.
(b) No population bill, as the General Assembly shall define by general law, shall be passed. No bill using classification by population as a means of determining the applicability of any bill or law to any political subdivision or group of political subdivisions may expressly or impliedly amend, modify, supersede, or repeal the general law defining a population bill.
(c) No special law relating to the rights or status of private persons shall be enacted.

Paragraph V. Specific limitations

(a) The General Assembly shall not have the power to grant incorporation to private persons but shall provide by general law the manner in which private corporate powers and privileges may be granted.

(b) The General Assembly shall not forgive the forfeiture of the charter of any corporation existing on August 13, 1945, nor shall it grant any benefit to or permit any amendment to the charter of any corporation except upon the condition that the acceptance thereof shall operate as a novation of the charter and that such corporation shall thereafter hold its charter subject to the provisions of this Constitution.

(c)(1) The General Assembly shall not have the power to authorize any contract or agreement which may have the effect of or which is intended to have the effect of encouraging a monopoly, which is hereby declared to be unlawful and void. Except as otherwise provided in subparagraph

(c)(2) of this Paragraph, the General Assembly shall not have the power to authorize any contract or agreement which may have the effect of or which is intended to have the effect of defeating or lessening competition, which is hereby declared to be unlawful and void.

(2) The General Assembly shall have the power to authorize and provide by general law for judicial enforcement of contracts or agreements restricting or regulating competitive activities between or among:

(A) Employers and employees;
(B) Distributors and manufacturers;
(C) Lessors and lessees;
(D) Partnerships and partners;
(E) Franchisors and franchisees;
(F) Sellers and purchasers of a business or commercial enterprise; or
(G) Two or more employers.

(3) The authority granted to the General Assembly in subparagraph (c)(2) of this Paragraph shall include the authority to grant to courts by general law the power to limit the duration, geographic area, and scope of prohibited activities provided in a contract or agreement restricting or regulating competitive activities to render such contract or agreement reasonable under the circumstances for which it was made.

(d) The General Assembly shall not have the power to regulate or fix charges of public utilities owned or operated by any county or municipality of this state, except as authorized by this Constitution.

(e) No municipal or county authority which is authorized to construct, improve, or maintain any road or street on behalf of, pursuant to a contract with, or through the use of taxes or other revenues of a county or municipal corporation shall be created by any local Act or pursuant to any general Act nor shall any law specifically relating to any such authority be amended unless the creation of such authority or the amendment of such law is conditioned upon the approval of a majority of the qualified voters of the county or municipal corporation affected voting in a referendum thereon. This subparagraph shall not apply to or affect any state authority.

Paragraph VI. Gratuities

(a) Except as otherwise provided in the Constitution,

(1) the General Assembly shall not have the power to grant any donation or gratuity or to forgive any debt or obligation owing to the public, and

(2) the General Assembly shall not grant or authorize extra compensation to any public officer, agent, or contractor after the service has been rendered or the contract entered into.

(b) All laws heretofore adopted under Article III, Section VIII, Paragraph XII of the Constitution of 1976 in force and effect on June 30, 1983, shall continue in force and effect and may be amended if such amendments are consistent with the authority granted to the General Assembly by such provisions of said Constitution.

(c) The General Assembly may provide by law and may expend or authorize the expenditure of public funds for a health insurance plan or program for persons and the spouses and dependent children of persons who are retired former employees of public schools or public school systems of this state.

(d) The General Assembly may provide by law for indemnification with respect to licensed emergency management rescue specialists who are or have been killed or permanently disabled in the line of duty on or after January 1, 1991, and publicly employed emergency medical technicians who are or have been killed or permanently disabled in the line of duty on or after January 1, 1987.

(e)(1) The General Assembly may provide by law for a program of indemnification with respect to the death or permanent disability of any law enforcement officer, fireman, prison guard, or publicly employed emergency medical technician who is or at any time in the past was killed or permanently disabled in the line of duty. Funds shall be appropriated as necessary for payment of such indemnification or for the purchase of insurance for such indemnification or both.

(2) The General Assembly may provide by law for a program of compensation for injuries incurred by law enforcement officers and firemen in the line of duty. A law enforcement officer who becomes physically disabled, but not permanently disabled, as a result of a physical injury incurred in the line of duty and caused by a willful act of violence and a fireman who becomes physically disabled, but not permanently disabled, as a result of a physical injury incurred in the line of duty while fighting a fire shall be entitled to receive monthly compensation from the state in an amount equal to any such person's regular compensation for the period of time that the law enforcement officer or fireman is physically unable to perform the duties of his or her employment; provided, however, that such benefits provided in this subparagraph shall not be granted for more than a total of 12 months for injuries resulting from a single incident. A law enforcement officer or fireman shall be required to submit to a state agency satisfactory evidence of such disability. Benefits made available under this subparagraph shall be subordinate to workers' compensation benefits, disability and other compensation benefits from an employer which the law enforcement officer or fireman is awarded and shall be limited to the difference between the amount of workers' compensation benefits, disability and other compensation benefits actually paid and the amount of the law enforcement officer's or fireman's regular compensation. Any law enforcement officer or fireman who receives indemnification under subparagraph (1) of this subparagraph (e) shall not be entitled to any compensation under this subparagraph.

(f) The General Assembly is authorized to provide by law for compensating innocent victims of crimes which occur on and after July 1, 1989. The General Assembly is authorized to define the types of victims eligible to receive compensation and to vary the amounts of compensation according to need. The General Assembly shall be authorized to allocate certain funds, to appropriate funds, to provide for a continuing fund, or to provide for any combination thereof for the purpose of compensating innocent victims of crime and for the administration of any laws enacted for such purpose.
(g) The General Assembly may provide by law for indemnification with respect to public school teachers, administrators, and employees who are killed or permanently disabled by an act of violence in the line of duty, a nonlapsing indemnification fund for such purposes, and dedication of revenue from special and distinctive motor vehicle license plates honoring Georgia educators to such fund.
(h) The General Assembly may provide by law for a program of indemnification with respect to the death or permanent disability of any state highway employee who is or at any time in the past was killed or permanently disabled in the line of duty. Funds shall be appropriated as necessary for payment of such indemnification or for the purchase of insurance for such indemnification or both.

Paragraph VII. Regulation of alcoholic beverages
The State of Georgia shall have full and complete authority to regulate alcoholic beverages and to regulate, restrict, or prohibit activities involving alcoholic beverages. This regulatory authority of the state shall include all such regulatory authority as is

permitted to the states under the Twenty-First Amendment to the United States Constitution. This regulatory authority of the state is specifically delegated to the counties and municipalities of the state for the purpose of regulating, restricting, or prohibiting the exhibition of nudity, partial nudity, or depictions of nudity in connection with the sale or consumption of alcoholic beverages; and such delegated regulatory authority may be exercised by the adoption and enforcement of regulatory ordinances by the counties and municipalities of this state. A general law exercising such regulatory authority shall control over conflicting provisions of any local ordinance but shall not preempt any local ordinance provisions not in direct conflict with general law.

SECTION VII. IMPEACHMENTS

Paragraph I. Power to impeach
The House of Representatives shall have the sole power to vote impeachment charges against any executive or judicial officer of this state or any member of the General Assembly.

Paragraph II. Trial of impeachments
The Senate shall have the sole power to try impeachments. When sitting for that purpose, the Senators shall be on oath, or affirmation, and shall be presided over by the Chief Justice of the Supreme Court. Should the Chief Justice be disqualified, then the Presiding Justice shall preside. Should the Presiding Justice be disqualified, then the Senate shall select a Justice of the Supreme Court to preside. No person shall be convicted without concurrence of two-thirds of the members to which the Senate is entitled.

Paragraph III. Judgments in impeachment
In cases of impeachment, judgments shall not extend further than removal from office and disqualification to hold and enjoy any office of honor, trust, or profit within this state or to receive a pension therefrom, but no such judgment shall relieve any party from any criminal or civil liability.

SECTION VIII. INSURANCE REGULATION

Paragraph I. Regulation of insurance
Provision shall be made by law for the regulation of insurance.
Paragraph II. Issuance of licenses. Insurance licenses shall be issued by the Commissioner of Insurance as required by law.

SECTION IX. APPROPRIATIONS

Paragraph I. Public money, how drawn
No money shall be drawn from the treasury except by appropriation made by law.

Paragraph II. Preparation, submission, and enactments of general appropriations bill

(a) The Governor shall submit to the General Assembly within five days after its convening in regular session each year a budget message and a budget report, accompanied by a draft of a general appropriations bill, in such form and manner as may be prescribed by statute, which shall provide for the appropriation of the funds necessary to operate all the various departments and agencies and to meet the current expenses of the state for the next fiscal year.
(b) The General Assembly shall annually appropriate those state and federal funds necessary to operate all the various departments and agencies. To the extent that federal funds received by the state for any program, project, activity, purpose, or expenditure are changed by federal authority or exceed the amount or amounts appropriated in the general appropriations Act or supplementary appropriation Act or Acts, or are not anticipated, such excess, changed or unanticipated federal funds are hereby continually appropriated for the purposes authorized and directed by the federal government in making the grant. In those instances where the conditions under which the federal funds have been made available do not provide otherwise, federal funds shall first be used to replace state funds that were appropriated to supplant federal funds in the same state fiscal

year. The fiscal year of the state shall commence on the first day of July of each year and terminate on the thirtieth of June following.

(c) The General Assembly shall by general law provide for the regulation and management of the finance and fiscal administration of the state.

Paragraph III. General appropriations bill

The general appropriations bill shall embrace nothing except appropriations fixed by previous laws; the ordinary expenses of the executive, legislative, and judicial departments of the government; payment of the public debt and interest thereon; and for support of the public institutions and educational interests of the state. All other appropriations shall be made by separate bills, each embracing but one subject.

Paragraph IV. General appropriations Act

(a) Each general appropriations Act, now of force or hereafter adopted with such amendments as are adopted from time to time, shall continue in force and effect for the next fiscal year after adoption and it shall then expire, except for the mandatory appropriations required by this Constitution and those required to meet contractual obligations authorized by this Constitution and the continued appropriation of federal grants.

(b) The General Assembly shall not appropriate funds for any given fiscal year which, in aggregate, exceed a sum equal to the amount of unappropriated surplus expected to have accrued in the state treasury at the beginning of the fiscal year together with an amount not greater than the total treasury receipts from existing revenue sources anticipated to be collected in the fiscal year, less refunds, as estimated in the budget report and amendments thereto. Supplementary appropriations, if any, shall be made in the manner provided in Paragraph V of this section of the Constitution; but in no event shall a supplementary appropriations Act continue in force and effect beyond the expiration of the general appropriations Act in effect when such

supplementary appropriations Act was adopted and approved.
(c) All appropriated state funds, except for the mandatory appropriations required by this Constitution, remaining unexpended and not contractually obligated at the expiration of such general appropriations Act shall lapse.
(d) Funds appropriated to or received by the State Housing Trust Fund for the Homeless shall not be subject to the provisions of Article III, Section IX, Paragraph IV(c), relative to the lapsing of funds, and may be expended for programs of purely public charity for the homeless, including programs involving the participation of churches and religious institutions, notwithstanding the provisions of Article I, Section II, Paragraph VII.

Paragraph V. Other or supplementary appropriations
In addition to the appropriations made by the general appropriations Act and amendments thereto, the General Assembly may make additional appropriations by Acts, which shall be known as supplementary appropriation Acts, provided no such supplementary appropriation shall be available unless there is an unappropriated surplus in the state treasury or the revenue necessary to pay such appropriation shall have been provided by a tax laid for such purpose and collected into the general fund of the state treasury. Neither house shall pass a supplementary appropriation bill until the general appropriations Act shall have been finally adopted by both houses and approved by the Governor.

Paragraph VI. Appropriations to be for specific sums

(a) Except as hereinafter provided, the appropriation for each department, officer, bureau, board, commission, agency, or institution for which appropriation is made shall be for a specific sum of money; and no appropriation shall allocate to any object the proceeds of any particular tax or fund or a part or percentage thereof.

(b) An amount equal to all money derived from motor fuel taxes received by the state in each of the immediately preceding fiscal years, less the amount of refunds, rebates, and collection costs authorized by law, is hereby appropriated for the fiscal year beginning July 1, of each year following, for all activities incident to providing and maintaining an adequate system of public roads and bridges in this state, as authorized by laws enacted by the General Assembly of Georgia, and for grants to counties by law authorizing road construction and maintenance, as provided by law authorizing such grants. Said sum is hereby appropriated for, and shall be available for, the aforesaid purposes regardless of whether the General Assembly enacts a general appropriations Act; and said sum need not be specifically stated in any general appropriations Act passed by the General Assembly in order to be available for such purposes. However, this shall not preclude the General Assembly from appropriating for such purposes an amount greater than the sum specified above for such purposes. The expenditure of such funds shall be subject to all the rules, regulations, and restrictions imposed on the expenditure of appropriations by provisions of the Constitution and laws of this state, unless such provisions are in conflict with the provisions of this paragraph. And provided, however, that the proceeds of the tax hereby appropriated shall not be subject to budgetary reduction. In the event of invasion of this state by land, sea, or air or in case of a major catastrophe so proclaimed by the Governor, said funds may be utilized for defense or relief purposes on the executive order of the Governor.

(c) A trust fund for use in the reimbursement of a portion of an employer's workers' compensation expenses resulting to an employee from the combination of a previous disability with subsequent injury incurred in employment may be provided for by law. As authorized by law, revenues raised for purposes of the fund may be paid into and disbursed from the trust without being subject to the limitations of subparagraph (a) of this Paragraph or of Article VII, Section III, Paragraph II.

(d) As provided by law, additional penalties may be assessed in any case in which any court in this state imposes a fine or orders the forfeiture of any bond in the nature of the penalty for all offenses against the criminal and traffic laws of this state or of the political subdivisions of this state. The proceeds derived from such additional penalty assessments may be allocated for the specific purpose of meeting any and all costs, or any portion of the cost, of providing training to law enforcement officers and to prosecuting officials.

(e) The General Assembly may by general law approved by a three-fifths' vote of both houses designate any part or all of the proceeds of any state tax now or hereafter levied and collected on alcoholic beverages to be used for prevention, education, and treatment relating to alcohol and drug abuse.

(f) The General Assembly is authorized to provide by law for the creation of a State Children's Trust Fund from which funds shall be disbursed for child abuse and neglect prevention programs. The General Assembly is authorized to appropriate moneys to such fund and such moneys paid into the fund shall not be subject to the provisions of Article III, Section IX, Paragraph IV(c), relative to the lapsing of funds.

(g) The General Assembly is authorized to provide by law for the creation of a Seed-Capital Fund from which funds shall be disbursed at the direction of the Advanced Technology Development Center of the University System of Georgia to provide equity and other capital to small, young, entrepreneurial firms engaged in innovative work in the areas of technology, manufacturing, or agriculture. Funds shall be disbursed in the form of loans or investments which shall provide for repayment, rents, dividends, royalties, or other forms of return on investments as provided by law. Moneys received from returns on loans or investments shall be deposited in the Seed-Capital Fund for further disbursement. The General Assembly is authorized to appropriate moneys to such fund and such moneys paid into the fund shall not be subject to the provisions of Article III, Section IX, Paragraph IV(c) relative to the lapsing of funds. The General Assembly shall be authorized to provide by law for any matters relating to the purpose or provisions of this subparagraph.

(h) The General Assembly is authorized to provide by general law for additional penalties or fees in any case in any court in this state in which a person is adjudged guilty of an offense against the criminal or traffic laws of this state or an ordinance of a political subdivision of this state. The General Assembly is authorized to provide by general law for the allocation of such additional penalties or fees for the construction, operation, and staffing of jails, correctional institutions, and detention facilities by counties.

(i) The General Assembly is authorized to provide by general law for the creation of an Indigent Care Trust Fund. Any hospital, hospital authority, county, or municipality is authorized to contribute or transfer moneys to the fund and any other person or entity specified by the General Assembly may also contribute to the fund. The General Assembly may provide by general law for the dedication and deposit of revenues raised from specified sources for the purposes of the fund into the fund. Moneys in the fund shall be exclusively used for primary health care programs for medically indigent citizens and children of this state, for expansion of Medicaid eligibility and services, or for programs to support rural and other health care providers, primarily hospitals, who disproportionately serve the medically indigent. Any other appropriation from the Indigent Care Trust Fund shall be void. Contributions and revenues deposited to the fund shall not lapse and shall not be subject to the limitations of subparagraph (a) of this Paragraph or of Article VII, Section III, Paragraph II. Contributions in the fund which are not appropriated as required by this subparagraph shall be refunded pro rata to the contributors thereof, as provided by the General Assembly.

(j) The General Assembly is authorized to provide by general law for the creation of an emerging crops fund from which to pay interest on loans made to farmers to enable such farmers to produce certain crops on Georgia farms and thereby promote economic development. The General Assembly is authorized to appropriate moneys to such fund and moneys so appropriated shall not be subject to the provisions of Article III, Section IX, Paragraph IV(c), relative to the lapsing of appropriated funds. Interest on loans made to farmers shall be paid from such fund pursuant to such terms, conditions, and requirements as the General Assembly shall provide by general law. The General Assembly may provide by general law for the administration of such fund by such state agency or public authority as the General Assembly shall determine.

(k) The General Assembly is authorized to provide by general law for additional penalties or fees in any case in any court in this state in which a person is adjudged guilty of an offense involving driving under the influence of alcohol or drugs or reckless driving. The General Assembly is authorized to provide by general law for the allocation of such additional penalties or fees to the Brain and Spinal Injury Trust Fund, as provided by law, for the specified purpose of meeting any and all costs, or any portion of the costs, of providing care and rehabilitative services to citizens of the state who have survived neurotrauma with head or spinal cord injuries. Moneys appropriated for such purposes shall not lapse. The General Assembly may provide by general law for the administration of such fund by such authority as the General Assembly shall determine.

(l) The General Assembly is authorized to provide by general law for the creation of a roadside enhancement and beautification fund from which funds shall be disbursed for enhancement and beautification of public rights of way; for allocation and dedication of revenue from tree and other vegetation trimming or removal permit fees, other related assessments, and special and distinctive wildflower motor vehicle license plate fees to such fund; that moneys paid into the fund shall not lapse, the provisions of Article III, Section IX, Paragraph IV(c) notwithstanding; and for any matters relating to the purpose or provisions of this subparagraph. An Act creating such fund and making such provisions effective January 1, 1999, or later may originate or have originated in the Senate or the House of Representatives.

(m) There shall be within the Department of Agriculture a dog and cat reproductive sterilization support program to control dog and cat overpopulation and thereby reduce the number of animals housed and killed in animal shelters, which program shall be administered by the Commissioner of Agriculture. In order to fund the program, there shall be issued beginning in 2003 specially designed license plates promoting the program. The General Assembly shall provide by law for the issuance of such license plates and for dedication of certain revenue derived from fees for such plates to the support of the program. All such dedicated revenue derived from special license plate fees, any funds appropriated to the department for such purposes, and any voluntary contributions or other funds made available to the department for such purposes and all interest thereon shall be deposited in a special fund for support of the program, shall not be used for any purpose other than support of the program, and shall not lapse. The General Assembly may provide by law for all matters necessary or appropriate to the implementation of this paragraph.

(n) The General Assembly may provide by law for the issuance and renewal of special motor vehicle license plates that motor vehicle owners may optionally purchase and renew for additional fees. The General Assembly may provide for all or a portion of the net revenue, as defined by the General Assembly, derived from the additional fees charged for any such special license plate to be dedicated to an agency, fund, or nonprofit corporation to implement or support programs related to the nature of the special license plate, as intended by the authorizing statute. Any dedication of funds enacted pursuant to the authority of this subparagraph may be in whole or in part for the ultimate use of a nonprofit corporation, without limitation by Article III, Section VI, Paragraph VI, if the General Assembly determines that the license plate program and such appropriation will benefit both the state and the nonprofit corporation. Any law enacted pursuant to the authority of this subparagraph may provide that funds dedicated pursuant to such law shall not lapse as otherwise required by Article III, Section IX, Paragraph IV(c). Any law enacted pursuant to the authority of this subparagraph shall be required to receive a two thirds' majority vote in both the Senate and the House of Representatives.

(o) The General Assembly may provide by general law for additional penalties in any case in any court in this state in which a person is adjudged guilty of keeping a place of prostitution, pimping, pandering, pandering by compulsion, solicitation of sodomy, masturbation for hire, trafficking of persons for sexual servitude, or sexual exploitation of children and may impose assessments on adult entertainment establishments as defined by law; and such appropriated amount shall not lapse as required by Article III, Section IX, Paragraph IV(c) and shall not be subject to the limitations of subparagraph (a) of this Paragraph, Article III, Section V, Paragraph II, Article VII, Section III, Paragraph II(a), or Article VII, Section III, Paragraph IV. The General Assembly may provide by general law for the allocation of such assessments and additional penalties to the Safe Harbor for Sexually Exploited Children Fund for the specified purpose of meeting any and all costs, or any portion of the costs, of providing care and rehabilitative and social services to individuals in this state who have been or may be sexually exploited. The General Assembly may provide by general law for the administration of such fund by such authority as the General Assembly shall determine.

(p) The proceeds of any excise tax imposed by general law on the sale of fireworks or consumer fireworks in this state shall be dedicated to the provision of trauma care, fire services, and local public safety purposes in Georgia. The General Assembly shall provide by general law for the use, dedication, and deposit of revenues raised from any such excise tax on fireworks or consumer fireworks. Contributions and revenues deposited for such purposes shall not lapse and shall not be subject to the limitations of subparagraph (a) of this Paragraph or of Article VII, Section III, Paragraph II.

Paragraph VII. Appropriations void, when
Any appropriation made in conflict with any of the foregoing provisions shall be void.

SECTION X. RETIREMENT SYSTEMS

Paragraph I. Expenditure of public funds authorized

Public funds may be expended for the purpose of paying benefits and other costs of retirement and pension systems for public officers and employees and their beneficiaries.

Paragraph II. Increasing benefits authorized

Public funds may be expended for the purpose of increasing benefits being paid pursuant to any retirement or pension system wholly or partially supported from public funds.

Paragraph III. Retirement systems covering employees of county boards of education

Notwithstanding Article IX, Section II, Paragraph III(a)(14), the authority to establish or modify heretofore existing local retirement systems covering employees of county boards of education shall continue to be vested in the General Assembly.

Paragraph IV. Firemen's Pension System

The powers of taxation may be exercised by the state through the General Assembly and the counties and municipalities for the purpose of paying pensions and other benefits and costs under a firemen's pension system or systems. The taxes so levied may be collected by such firemen's pension system or systems and disbursed therefrom by authority of the General Assembly for the purposes therein authorized.

Paragraph V. Funding standards

It shall be the duty of the General Assembly to enact legislation to define funding standards which will assure the actuarial soundness of any retirement or pension system supported wholly or partially from public funds and to control legislative procedures so that no bill or resolution creating or amending any such retirement or pension system shall be passed by the General Assembly without concurrent provisions for funding in accordance with the defined funding standards.

Paragraph V-A. Limitation on involuntary separation benefits for Governor of the State of Georgia
Any other provisions of this Constitution to the contrary notwithstanding, no past, present, or future Governor of the State of Georgia who ceases or ceased to hold office as Governor for any reason, except for medical disability, shall receive a retirement benefit based on involuntary separation from employment as a result of ceasing to hold office as Governor. The provisions of any law in conflict with this Paragraph are null and void effective January 1, 1985.

Paragraph VI. Involuntary separation; part-time service

(a) Any public retirement or pension system provided for by law in existence prior to January 1, 1985, may be changed by the General Assembly for any one or more of the following purposes:
(1) To redefine involuntary separation from employment; or
(2) To provide additional or revise existing limitations or restrictions on the right to qualify for a retirement benefit based on involuntary separation from employment.

(b) The General Assembly by law may define or redefine part-time service, including but not limited to service as a member of the General Assembly, for the purposes of any public retirement or pension system presently existing or created in the future and may limit or restrict the use of such part-time service as creditable service under any such retirement or pension system.
(c) Any law enacted by the General Assembly pursuant to subparagraph (a) or (b) of this Paragraph may affect persons who are members of public retirement or pension systems on January 1, 1985, and who became members at any time prior to that date.
(d) Any law enacted by the General Assembly pursuant to subparagraph (a) or (b) of this Paragraph shall not be subject to any law controlling legislative procedures for the consideration of retirement or pension bills, including, but not limited to, any limitations on the sessions of the General Assembly at which retirement or pension bills may be introduced.

(e) No public retirement or pension system created on or after January 1, 1985, shall grant any person whose retirement is based on involuntary separation from employment a retirement or pension benefit more favorable than the retirement or pension benefit granted to a person whose separation from employment is voluntary.

ARTICLE IV: CONSTITUTIONAL BOARDS AND COMMISSIONS

SECTION I. PUBLIC SERVICE COMMISSION

Paragraph I. Public Service Commission

(a) There shall be a Public Service Commission for the regulation of utilities which shall consist of five members who shall be elected by the people. The Commissioners in office on June 30, 1983, shall serve until December 31 after the general election at which the successor of each member is elected. Thereafter, all succeeding terms of members shall be for six years. Members shall serve until their successors are elected and qualified. A chairman shall be selected by the members of the commission from its membership.
(b) The commission shall be vested with such jurisdiction, powers, and duties as provided by law. The filling of vacancies and manner and time of election of members of the commission shall be as provided by law.

SECTION II. STATE BOARD OF PARDONS AND PAROLES

Paragraph I. State Board of Pardons and Paroles
There shall be a State Board of Pardons and Paroles which shall consist of five members appointed by the Governor, subject to confirmation by the Senate. The members of the board in office on June 30, 1983, shall serve out the remainder of their respective terms, provided that the expiration date of the term of any such member shall be December 31 of the year in which the member's term expires. As each term of office expires, the Governor shall appoint a successor as herein provided. All such terms of members shall be for seven years. A chairman shall be selected by the members of the board from its membership.

Paragraph II. Powers and authority

(a) Except as otherwise provided in this Paragraph, the State Board of Pardons and Paroles shall be vested with the power of executive clemency, including the powers to grant reprieves, pardons, and paroles; to commute penalties; to remove disabilities imposed by law; and to remit any part of a sentence for any offense against the state after conviction.

(b)(1) When a sentence of death is commuted to life imprisonment, the board shall not have the authority to grant a pardon to the convicted person until such person has served at least 25 years in the penitentiary; and such person shall not become eligible for parole at any time prior to serving at least 25 years in the penitentiary.

(2) The General Assembly may by general law approved by two-thirds of the members elected to each branch of the General Assembly in a roll-call vote provide for minimum mandatory sentences and for sentences which are required to be served in their entirety for persons convicted of armed robbery, kidnapping, rape, aggravated child molestation, aggravated sodomy, or aggravated sexual battery and, when so provided by such Act, the board shall not have the authority to consider such persons for pardon, parole, or commutation during that portion of the sentence.

(3) The General Assembly may by general law approved by two-thirds of the members elected to each branch of the General Assembly in a roll-call vote provide for the imposition of sentences of life without parole for persons convicted of murder and for persons who having been previously convicted of murder, armed robbery, kidnapping, rape, aggravated child molestation, aggravated sodomy, or aggravated sexual battery or having been previously convicted under the laws of any other state or of the United States of a crime which if committed in this state would be one of those offenses and who after such previous conviction subsequently commits and is convicted of one of those offenses and, when so provided by such Act, the board shall not have the authority to consider such persons for pardon, parole, or commutation from any portion of such sentence.

(4) Any general law previously enacted by the General Assembly providing for life without parole or for mandatory service of sentences without suspension, probation, or parole is hereby ratified and approved but such provisions shall be subject to amendment or repeal by general law.

(c) Notwithstanding the provisions of subparagraph (b) of this Paragraph, the General Assembly, by law, may prohibit the board from granting and may prescribe the terms and conditions for the board's granting a pardon or parole to:

(1) Any person incarcerated for a second or subsequent time for any offense for which such person could have been sentenced to life imprisonment; and
(2) Any person who has received consecutive life sentences as the result of offenses occurring during the same series of acts.

(d) The chairman of the board, or any other member designated by the board, may suspend the execution of a sentence of death until the full board shall have an opportunity to hear the application of the convicted person for any relief within the power of the board.
(e) Notwithstanding any other provisions of this Paragraph, the State Board of Pardons and Paroles shall have the authority to pardon any person convicted of a crime who is subsequently determined to be innocent of said crime or to issue a medical reprieve to an entirely incapacitated person suffering a progressively debilitating terminal illness or parole any person who is age 62 or older.

SECTION III. STATE PERSONNEL BOARD

Paragraph I. State Personnel Board

(a) There shall be a State Personnel Board which shall consist of five members appointed by the Governor, subject to confirmation by the Senate. The members of the board in office on June 30, 1983, shall serve out the remainder of their respective terms. As each term of office expires, the Governor shall appoint a successor as herein provided. All such terms of members shall be for five years. Members shall serve until their successors are appointed and qualified. A member of the State Personnel Board may not be employed in any other capacity in state government. A chairman shall be selected by the members of the board from its membership.

(b) The board shall provide policy direction for a State Merit System of Personnel Administration and may be vested with such additional powers and duties as provided by law. State personnel shall be selected on the basis of merit as provided by law. Paragraph II. Veterans preference. Any veteran who has served as a member of the armed forces of the United States during the period of a war or armed conflict in which any branch of the armed forces of the United States engaged, whether under United States command or otherwise, and was honorably discharged therefrom, shall be given such veterans preference in any civil service program established in state government as may be provided by law. Any such law must provide at least ten points to a veteran having at least a 10 percent service connected disability as rated and certified by the Veterans Administration, and all other such veterans shall be entitled to at least five points.

SECTION IV. STATE TRANSPORTATION BOARD

Paragraph I. State Transportation Board; commissioner

(a) There shall be a State Transportation Board composed of as many members as there are congressional districts in the state. The member of the board from each congressional district shall be elected by a majority vote of the members of the House of Representatives and Senate whose respective districts are embraced or partly embraced within such congressional district meeting in caucus. The members of the board in office on June 30, 1983, shall serve out the remainder of their respective terms. The General Assembly shall provide by law the procedure for the election of members and for filling vacancies on the board.

Members shall serve for terms of five years and until their successors are elected and qualified.

(b) The State Transportation Board shall select a commissioner of transportation, who shall be the chief executive officer of the Department of Transportation and who shall have such powers and duties as provided by law.

SECTION V. VETERANS SERVICE BOARD

Paragraph I. Veterans Service Board; commissioner

(a) There shall be a State Department of Veterans Service and Veterans Service Board which shall consist of seven members appointed by the Governor, subject to confirmation by the Senate. The members in office on June 30, 1983, shall serve out the remainder of their respective terms. As each term of office expires, the Governor shall appoint a successor as herein provided. All such terms of members shall be for seven years. Members shall serve until their successors are appointed and qualified.

(b) The board shall appoint a commissioner who shall be the executive officer of the department. All members of the board and the commissioner shall be veterans of some war or armed conflict in which the United States has engaged. The board shall have such control, duties, powers, and jurisdiction of the State Department of Veterans Service as shall be provided by law.

SECTION VI. BOARD OF NATURAL RESOURCES

Paragraph I. Board of Natural Resources

(a) There shall be a Board of Natural Resources which shall consist of one member from each congressional district in the state and five members from the state at large, one of whom must be from one of the following named counties: Chatham, Bryan, Liberty, McIntosh, Glynn, or Camden. All members shall be appointed by the Governor, subject to confirmation by the Senate. The members of the board in office on June 30, 1983,

shall serve out the remainder of their respective terms. As each term of office expires, the Governor shall appoint a successor as herein provided. All such terms of members shall be for seven years. Members shall serve until their successors are appointed and qualified. Insofar as it is practicable, the members of the board shall be representative of all areas and functions encompassed within the Department of Natural Resources.
(b) The board shall have such powers and duties as provided by law.

SECTION VII. QUALIFICATIONS, COMPENSATION, REMOVAL FROM OFFICE, AND POWERS AND DUTIES OF MEMBERS OF CONSTITUTIONAL BOARDS AND COMMISSIONS

Paragraph I. Qualifications, compensation, and removal from office
The qualifications, compensation, and removal from office of members of constitutional boards and commissions provided for in this article shall be as provided by law.

Paragraph II. Powers and duties
The powers and duties of members of constitutional boards and commissions provided for in this article, except the Board of Pardons and Paroles, shall be as provided by law.

ARTICLE V: EXECUTIVE BRANCH

SECTION I. ELECTION OF GOVERNOR AND LIEUTENANT GOVERNOR

Paragraph I. Governor: term of office; compensation and allowances

There shall be a Governor who shall hold office for a term of four years and until a successor shall be chosen and qualified. Persons holding the office of Governor may succeed themselves for one four-year term of office. Persons who have held the office of Governor and have succeeded themselves as hereinbefore provided shall not again be eligible to be elected to that office until after the expiration of four years from the conclusion of their term as Governor. The compensation and allowances of the Governor shall be as provided by law.

Paragraph II. Election for Governor

An election for Governor shall be held on Tuesday after the first Monday in November of 1986, and the Governor-elect shall be installed in office at the next session of the General Assembly. An election for Governor shall take place quadrennially thereafter on said date unless another date be fixed by the General Assembly. Said election shall be held at the places of holding general elections in the several counties of this state, in the manner prescribed for the election of members of the General Assembly, and the electors shall be the same.

Paragraph III. Lieutenant Governor

There shall be a Lieutenant Governor, who shall be elected at the same time, for the same term, and in the same manner as the Governor. The Lieutenant Governor shall be the President of the Senate and shall have such executive duties as prescribed by the Governor and as may be prescribed by law not inconsistent with the powers of the Governor or other provisions of this Constitution. The compensation and allowances of the Lieutenant Governor shall be as provided by law.

Paragraph IV. Qualifications of Governor and Lieutenant Governor

No person shall be eligible for election to the office of Governor or Lieutenant Governor unless such person shall have been a citizen of the United States 15 years and a legal resident of the state six years immediately preceding the election and shall have attained the age of 30 years by the date of assuming office.

Paragraph V. Succession to executive power.

(a) In case of the temporary disability of the Governor as determined in the manner provided in Section IV of this article, the Lieutenant Governor shall exercise the powers and duties of the Governor and receive the same compensation as the Governor until such time as the temporary disability of the Governor ends.

(b) In case of the death, resignation, or permanent disability of the Governor or the Governor-elect, the Lieutenant Governor or the Lieutenant Governor-elect, upon becoming the Lieutenant Governor, shall become the Governor until a successor shall be elected and qualified as hereinafter provided. A successor to serve for the unexpired term shall be elected at the next general election; but, if such death, resignation, or permanent disability shall occur within 30 days of the next general election or if the term will expire within 90 days after the next general election, the Lieutenant Governor shall become Governor for the unexpired term. No person shall be elected or appointed to the office of Lieutenant Governor for the unexpired term in the event the Lieutenant Governor shall become Governor as herein provided.

(c) In case of the death, resignation, or permanent disability of both the Governor or the Governor-elect and the Lieutenant Governor or the Lieutenant Governor-elect or in case of the death, resignation, or permanent disability of the Governor and there shall be no Lieutenant Governor, the Speaker of the House of Representatives shall exercise the powers and duties of the Governor until the election and qualification of a Governor at a special election, which shall be held within 90 days from the date on which the Speaker of the House of Representatives shall have assumed the powers and duties of the Governor, and the person elected shall serve out the unexpired term.

Paragraph VI. Oath of office
The Governor and Lieutenant Governor shall, before entering on the duties of office, take such oath or affirmation as prescribed by law.

SECTION II. DUTIES AND POWERS OF GOVERNOR

Paragraph I. Executive powers
The chief executive powers shall be vested in the Governor. The other executive officers shall have such powers as may be prescribed by this Constitution and by law.

Paragraph II. Law enforcement
The Governor shall take care that the laws are faithfully executed and shall be the conservator of the peace throughout the state.

Paragraph III. Commander in chief
The Governor shall be the commander in chief of the military forces of this state.

Paragraph IV. Veto power
Except as otherwise provided in this Constitution, before any bill or resolution shall become law, the Governor shall have the right to review such bill or resolution intended to have the effect of law which has been passed by the General Assembly. The Governor may veto, approve, or take no action on any such bill or resolution. In the event the Governor vetoes any such bill or resolution, the General Assembly may, by a two-thirds' vote, override such veto as provided in Article III of this Constitution. Paragraph V. Writs of election. The Governor shall issue writs of election to fill all vacancies that may occur in the Senate and in the House of Representatives.

Paragraph VI. Information and recommendations to the General Assembly

At the beginning of each regular session and from time to time, the Governor may give the General Assembly information on the state of the state and recommend to its consideration such measures as the Governor may deem necessary or expedient.

Paragraph VII. Special sessions of the General Assembly

(a) The Governor may convene the General Assembly in special session by proclamation which may be amended by the Governor prior to the convening of the special session or amended by the Governor with the approval of three-fifths of the members of each house after the special session has convened; but no laws shall be enacted at any such special session except those which relate to the purposes stated in the proclamation or in any amendment thereto.

(b) The Governor shall convene the General Assembly in special session for all purposes whenever three-fifths of the members to which each house is entitled certify to the Governor in writing, with a copy to the Secretary of State, that in their opinion an emergency exists in the affairs of the state. The General Assembly may convene itself if, after receiving such certification, the Governor fails to do so within three days, excluding Sundays.

(c) Special sessions of the General Assembly shall be limited to a period of 40 days unless extended by three-fifths' vote of each house and approved by the Governor or unless at the expiration of such period an impeachment trial of some officer of state government is pending, in which event the House shall adjourn and the Senate shall remain in session until such trial is completed.

Paragraph VIII. Filling vacancies

(a) When any public office shall become vacant by death, resignation, or otherwise, the Governor shall promptly fill such vacancy unless otherwise provided by this Constitution or by law; and persons so appointed shall serve for the unexpired term unless otherwise provided by this Constitution or by law.

(b) In case of the death or withdrawal of a person who received a majority of votes cast in an election for the office of Secretary of State, Attorney General, State School Superintendent, Commissioner of Insurance, Commissioner of Agriculture, or Commissioner of Labor, the Governor elected at the same election, upon becoming Governor, shall have the power to fill such office by appointing, subject to the confirmation of the Senate, an individual to serve until the next general election and until a successor for the balance of the unexpired term shall have been elected and qualified.

Paragraph IX. Appointments by Governor
The Governor shall make such appointments as are authorized by this Constitution or by law. If a person whose confirmation is required by the Senate is once rejected by the Senate, that person shall not be renominated by the Governor for appointment to the same office until the expiration of a period of one year from the date of such rejection.

Paragraph X. Information from officers and employees
The Governor may require information in writing from constitutional officers and all other officers and employees of the executive branch on any subject relating to the duties of their respective offices or employment.

SECTION III. OTHER ELECTED EXECUTIVE OFFICERS

Paragraph I. Other executive officers, how elected
The Secretary of State, Attorney General, State School Superintendent, Commissioner of Insurance, Commissioner of Agriculture, and Commissioner of Labor shall be elected in the manner prescribed for the election of members of the General Assembly and the electors shall be the same. Such executive officers shall be elected at the same time and hold their offices for the same term as the Governor.

Paragraph II. Qualifications

(a) No person shall be eligible to the office of the Secretary of State, Attorney General, State School Superintendent, Commissioner of Insurance, Commissioner of Agriculture, or Commissioner of Labor unless such person shall have been a citizen of the United States for ten years and a legal resident of the state for four years immediately preceding election or appointment and shall have attained the age of 25 years by the date of assuming office. All of said officers shall take such oath and give bond and security, as prescribed by law, for the faithful discharge of their duties.
(b) No person shall be Attorney General unless such person shall have been an active-status member of the State Bar of Georgia for seven years.

Paragraph III. Powers, duties, compensation, and allowances of other executive officers

Except as otherwise provided in this Constitution, the General Assembly shall prescribe the powers, duties, compensation, and allowances of the above executive officers and provide assistance and expenses necessary for the operation of the department of each.

Paragraph IV. Attorney General; duties

The Attorney General shall act as the legal advisor of the executive department, shall represent the state in the Supreme Court in all capital felonies and in all civil and criminal cases in any court when required by the Governor, and shall perform such other duties as shall be required by law.

SECTION IV. DISABILITY OF EXECUTIVE OFFICERS

Paragraph I. 'Elected constitutional executive officer,' how defined

As used in this section, the term 'elected constitutional executive officer' means the Governor, the Lieutenant Governor, the Secretary of State, the Attorney General, the State School

Superintendent, the Commissioner of Insurance, the Commissioner of Agriculture, and the Commissioner of Labor.

Paragraph II. Procedure for determining disability
Upon a petition of any four of the elected constitutional executive officers to the Supreme Court of Georgia that another elected constitutional executive officer is unable to perform the duties of office because of a physical or mental disability, the Supreme Court shall by appropriate rule provide for a speedy and public hearing on such matter, including notice of the nature and cause of the accusation, process for obtaining witnesses, and the assistance of counsel. Evidence at such hearing shall include testimony from not fewer than three qualified physicians in private practice, one of whom must be a psychiatrist.

Paragraph III. Effect of determination of disability
If, after hearing the evidence on disability, the Supreme Court determines that there is a disability and that such disability is permanent, the office shall be declared vacant and the successor to that office shall be chosen as provided in this Constitution or the laws enacted in pursuance thereof. If it is determined that the disability is not permanent, the Supreme Court shall determine when the disability has ended and when the officer shall resume the exercise of the powers of office. During the period of temporary disability, the powers of such office shall be exercised as provided by law.

ARTICLE VI: JUDICIAL BRANCH

SECTION I. JUDICIAL POWER

Paragraph I. Judicial power of the state
The judicial power of the state shall be vested exclusively in the following classes of courts: magistrate courts, probate courts, juvenile courts, state courts, superior courts, Court of Appeals, and Supreme Court. Magistrate courts, probate courts, juvenile courts, and state courts shall be courts of limited jurisdiction. In addition, the General Assembly may establish or authorize the establishment of municipal courts and may authorize administrative agencies to exercise quasi-judicial powers. Municipal courts shall have jurisdiction over ordinance violations and such other jurisdiction as provided by law. Except as provided in this paragraph and in Section X, municipal courts, county recorder's courts and civil courts in existence on June 30, 1983, and administrative agencies shall not be subject to the provisions of this article. The General Assembly shall have the authority to confer 'by law' jurisdiction upon municipal courts to try state offenses.

Paragraph II. Unified judicial system
All courts of the state shall comprise a unified judicial system.

Paragraph III. Judges; exercise of power outside own court; scope of term 'judge'
Provided the judge is otherwise qualified, a judge may exercise judicial power in any court upon the request and with the consent of the judges of that court and of the judge's own court under rules prescribed by law. The term 'judge,' as used in this article, shall include Justices, judges, senior judges, magistrates, and every other such judicial office of whatever name existing or created.

Paragraph IV. Exercise of judicial power
Each court may exercise such powers as necessary in aid of its jurisdiction or to protect or effectuate its judgments; but only the superior and appellate courts shall have the power to issue process in the nature of mandamus, prohibition, specific performance, quo warranto, and injunction. Each superior court, state court, and other courts of record may grant new trials on legal grounds.

Paragraph V. Uniformity of jurisdiction, powers, etc
Except as otherwise provided in this Constitution, the courts of each class shall have uniform jurisdiction, powers, rules of practice and procedure, and selection, qualifications, terms, and discipline of judges. The provisions of this Paragraph shall be effected by law within 24 months of the effective date of this Constitution.

Paragraph VI. Judicial circuits; courts in each county; court sessions
The state shall be divided into judicial circuits, each of which shall consist of not less than one county. Each county shall have at least one superior court, magistrate court, a probate court, and, where needed, a state court and a juvenile court. The General Assembly may provide by law that the judge of the probate court may also serve as the judge of the magistrate court. In the absence of a state court or a juvenile court, the superior court shall exercise that jurisdiction. Superior courts shall hold court at least twice each year in each county.

Paragraph VII. Judicial circuits, courts, and judgeships, law changed
The General Assembly may abolish, create, consolidate, or modify judicial circuits and courts and judgeships; but no circuit shall consist of less than one county.

Paragraph VIII. Transfer of cases
Any court shall transfer to the appropriate court in the state any civil case in which it determines that jurisdiction or venue lies elsewhere.

Paragraph IX. Rules of evidence; law prescribed. All rules of evidence shall be as prescribed by law

Paragraph X. Authorization for pilot projects
The General Assembly may by general law approved by a two-thirds' majority of the members of each house enact legislation providing for, as pilot programs of limited duration, courts which are not uniform within their classes in jurisdiction, powers, rules of practice and procedure, and selection, qualifications, terms, and discipline of judges for such pilot courts and other matters relative thereto. Such legislation shall name the political subdivision, judicial circuit, and existing courts affected and may, in addition to any other power, grant to such court created as a pilot program the power to issue process in the nature of mandamus, prohibition, specific performance, quo warranto, and injunction. The General Assembly shall provide by general law for a procedure for submitting proposed legislation relating to such pilot programs to the Judicial Council of Georgia or its successor. Legislation enacted pursuant to this Paragraph shall not deny equal protection of the laws to any person in violation of Article I, Section I, Paragraph II of this Constitution.

SECTION II. VENUE

Paragraph I. Divorce cases
Divorce cases shall be tried in the county where the defendant resides, if a resident of this state; if the defendant is not a resident of this state, then in the county in which the plaintiff resides; provided, however, a divorce case may be tried in the county of residence of the plaintiff if the defendant has moved from that same county within six months from the date of the filing of the divorce action and said county was the site of the marital domicile at the time of the separation of the parties, and

provided, further, that any person who has been a resident of any United States army post or military reservation within the State of Georgia for one year next preceding the filing of the petition may bring an action for divorce in any county adjacent to said United States army post or military reservation.

Paragraph II. Land titles
Cases respecting titles to land shall be tried in the county where the land lies, except where a single tract is divided by a county line, in which case the superior court of either county shall have jurisdiction.

Paragraph III. Equity cases
Equity cases shall be tried in the county where a defendant resides against whom substantial relief is prayed.

Paragraph IV. Suits against joint obligors, copartners, etc
Suits against joint obligors, joint tort-feasors, joint promisors, copartners, or joint trespassers residing in different counties may be tried in either county.

Paragraph V. Suits against maker, endorser, etc
Suits against the maker and endorser of promissory notes, or drawer, acceptor, and endorser of foreign or inland bills of exchange, or like instruments, residing in different counties, shall be tried in the county where the maker or acceptor resides.

Paragraph VI. All other cases
All other civil cases, except juvenile court cases as may otherwise be provided by the Juvenile Court Code of Georgia, shall be tried in the county where the defendant resides; venue as to corporations, foreign and domestic, shall be as provided by law; and all criminal cases shall be tried in the county where the crime was committed, except cases in the superior courts where the judge is satisfied that an impartial jury cannot be obtained in such county.

Paragraph VII. Venue in third-party practice
The General Assembly may provide by law that venue is proper in a county other than the county of residence of a person or entity impleaded into a pending civil case by a defending party who contends that such person or entity is or may be liable to said defending party for all or part of the claim against said defending party.

Paragraph VIII. Power to change venue
The power to change the venue in civil and criminal cases shall be vested in the superior courts to be exercised in such manner as has been, or shall be, provided by law.

SECTION III. CLASSES OF COURTS OF LIMITED JURISDICTION

Paragraph I. Jurisdiction of classes of courts of limited jurisdiction
The magistrate, juvenile, and state courts shall have uniform jurisdiction as provided by law. Probate courts shall have such jurisdiction as now or hereafter provided by law, without regard to uniformity.

SECTION IV. SUPERIOR COURTS

Paragraph I. Jurisdiction of superior courts
The superior courts shall have jurisdiction in all cases, except as otherwise provided in this Constitution. They shall have exclusive jurisdiction over trials in felony cases, except in the case of juvenile offenders as provided by law; in cases respecting title to land; in divorce cases; and in equity cases. The superior courts shall have such appellate jurisdiction, either alone or by circuit or district, as may be provided by law.

SECTION V. COURT OF APPEALS

Paragraph I
Composition of Court of Appeals; Chief Judge. The Court of Appeals shall consist of not less than nine Judges who shall elect from among themselves a Chief Judge.

Paragraph II. Panels as prescribed
The Court of Appeals may sit in panels of not less than three Judges as prescribed by law or, if none, by its rules.

Paragraph III. Jurisdiction of Court of Appeals; decisions binding
The Court of Appeals shall be a court of review and shall exercise appellate and certiorari jurisdiction in all cases not reserved to the Supreme Court or conferred on other courts by law. The decisions of the Court of Appeals insofar as not in conflict with those of the Supreme Court shall bind all courts except the Supreme Court as precedents.

Paragraph IV. Certification of question to Supreme Court
The Court of Appeals may certify a question to the Supreme Court for instruction, to which it shall then be bound.
Paragraph V. Equal division of court. In the event of an equal division of the Judges when sitting as a body, the case shall be immediately transmitted to the Supreme Court.

SECTION VI. SUPREME COURT

Paragraph I. Composition of Supreme Court; Chief Justice; Presiding Justice; quorum; substitute judges
The Supreme Court shall consist of not more than nine Justices who shall elect from among themselves a Chief Justice as the chief presiding and administrative officer of the court and a Presiding Justice to serve if the Chief Justice is absent or is disqualified. A majority shall be necessary to hear and determine cases. If a Justice is disqualified in any case, a substitute judge may be designated by the remaining Justices to serve.

Paragraph II. Exclusive appellate jurisdiction of Supreme Court. The Supreme Court shall be a court of review and shall exercise exclusive appellate jurisdiction in the following cases:

(1) All cases involving the construction of a treaty or of the Constitution of the State of Georgia or of the United States and all cases in which the constitutionality of a law, ordinance, or constitutional provision has been drawn in question; and
(2) All cases of election contest.

Paragraph III. General appellate jurisdiction of Supreme Court

Unless otherwise provided by law, the Supreme Court shall have appellate jurisdiction of the following classes of cases:

(1) Cases involving title to land;
(2) All equity cases;
(3) All cases involving wills;
(4) All habeas corpus cases;
(5) All cases involving extraordinary remedies;
(6) All divorce and alimony cases;
(7) All cases certified to it by the Court of Appeals; and
(8) All cases in which a sentence of death was imposed or could be imposed. Review of all cases shall be as provided by law.
Paragraph IV. Jurisdiction over questions of law from state appellate or federal district or appellate courts. The Supreme Court shall have jurisdiction and authority to answer any question of law from any state appellate or federal district or appellate court.

Paragraph V. Review of cases in Court of Appeals

The Supreme Court may review by certiorari cases in the Court of Appeals which are of gravity or great public importance.

Paragraph VI. Decisions of Supreme Court binding

The decisions of the Supreme Court shall bind all other courts as precedents.

SECTION VII. SELECTION, TERM, COMPENSATION, AND DISCIPLINE OF JUDGES

Paragraph I. Election; term of office
All superior court and state court judges shall be elected on a nonpartisan basis for a term of four years. All Justices of the Supreme Court and the Judges of the Court of Appeals shall be elected on a nonpartisan basis for a term of six years. The terms of all judges thus elected shall begin the next January 1 after their election. All other judges shall continue to be selected in the manner and for the term they were selected on June 30, 1983, until otherwise provided by local law.

Paragraph II. Qualifications

(a) Appellate and superior court judges shall have been admitted to practice law for seven years.
(b) State court judges shall have been admitted to practice law for seven years, provided that this requirement shall be five years in the case of state court judges elected or appointed in the year 2000 or earlier. Juvenile court judges shall have been admitted to practice law for five years.
(c) Probate and magistrate judges shall have such qualifications as provided by law.
(d) All judges shall reside in the geographical area in which they are selected to serve.
(e) The General Assembly may provide by law for additional qualifications, including, but not limited to, minimum residency requirements.

Paragraph III. Vacancies
Vacancies shall be filled by appointment of the Governor except as otherwise provided by law in the magistrate, probate, and juvenile courts.

Paragraph IV. Period of service of appointees
An appointee to an elective office shall serve until a successor is duly selected and qualified and until January 1 of the year following the next general election which is more than six months after such person's appointment.

Paragraph V. Compensation and allowances of judges
All judges shall receive compensation and allowances as provided by law; county supplements are hereby continued and may be granted or changed by the General Assembly. County governing authorities which had the authority on June 30, 1983, to make county supplements shall continue to have such authority under this Constitution. An incumbent's salary, allowance, or supplement shall not be decreased during the incumbent's term of office.

Paragraph VI. Judicial Qualifications Commission; power; composition

(a) The General Assembly shall by general law create and provide for the composition, manner of appointment, and governance of a Judicial Qualifications Commission, with such commission having the power to discipline, remove, and cause involuntary retirement of judges as provided by this Article. Appointments to the Judicial Qualifications Commission shall be subject to confirmation by the Senate as provided for by general law.
(b) The procedures of the Judicial Qualifications Commission shall comport with due process. Such procedures and advisory opinions issued by the Judicial Qualifications Commission shall be subject to review by the Supreme Court. -37
(c) The Judicial Qualifications Commission which existed on June 30, 2017, is hereby abolished.

Paragraph VII. Discipline, removal, and involuntary retirement of judges

(a) Any judge may be removed, suspended, or otherwise disciplined for willful misconduct in office, or for willful and persistent failure to perform the duties of office, or for habitual intemperance, or for conviction of a crime involving moral turpitude, or for conduct prejudicial to the administration of justice which brings the judicial office into disrepute. Any judge may be retired for disability which constitutes a serious and likely permanent interference with the performance of the duties of office. The Supreme Court shall adopt rules of implementation.
(b)(1) Upon indictment for a felony by a grand jury of this state or by a grand jury of the United States of any judge, the Attorney General or district attorney shall transmit a certified copy of the indictment to the Judicial Qualifications Commission. The commission shall, subject to subparagraph
(b)(2) of this Paragraph, review the indictment, and, if it determines that the indictment relates to and adversely affects the administration of the office of the indicted judge and that the rights and interests of the public are adversely affected thereby, the commission shall suspend the judge immediately and without further action pending the final disposition of the case or until the expiration of the judge's term of office, whichever occurs first. During the term of office to which such judge was elected and in which the indictment occurred, if a nolle prosequi is entered, if the public official is acquitted, or if after conviction the conviction is later overturned as a result of any direct appeal or application for a writ of certiorari, the judge shall be immediately reinstated to the office from which he was suspended. While a judge is suspended under this subparagraph and until initial conviction by the trial court, the judge shall continue to receive the compensation from his office. After initial conviction by the trial court, the judge shall not be entitled to receive the compensation from his office. If the judge is reinstated to office, he shall be entitled to receive any compensation withheld under the provisions of this subparagraph. For the duration of any suspension under this subparagraph, the Governor shall appoint

a replacement judge. Upon a final conviction with no appeal or review pending, the office shall be declared vacant and a successor to that office shall be chosen as provided in this Constitution or the laws enacted in pursuance thereof.

(2) The commission shall not review the indictment for a period of 14 days from the day the indictment is received. This period of time may be extended by the commission. During this period of time, the indicted judge may, in writing, authorize the commission to suspend him from office. Any such voluntary suspension shall be subject to the same conditions for review, reinstatement, or declaration of vacancy as are provided in this subparagraph for a nonvoluntary suspension.
(3) After any suspension is imposed under this subparagraph, the suspended judge may petition the commission for a review. If the commission determines that the judge should no longer be suspended, he shall immediately be reinstated to office.
(4)(A) The findings and records of the commission and the fact that the public official has or has not been suspended shall not be admissible in evidence in any court for any purpose.
(B) The findings and records of the commission shall not be open to the public except as provided by the General Assembly by general law.

(5) The provisions of this subparagraph shall not apply to any indictment handed down prior to January 1, 1985. (6) If a judge who is suspended from office under the provisions of this subparagraph is not first tried at the next regular or special term following the indictment, the suspension shall be terminated and the judge shall be reinstated to office. The judge shall not be reinstated under this provision if he is not so tried based on a continuance granted upon a motion made only by the defendant.

(c) Upon initial conviction of any judge for any felony in a trial court of this state or the United States, regardless of whether the judge has been suspended previously under subparagraph (b) of this Paragraph, such judge shall be immediately and without further action suspended from office. While a judge is suspended from office under this subparagraph, he shall not be entitled to receive the compensation from his office. If the conviction is later overturned as a result of any direct appeal or application for a writ of certiorari, the judge shall be immediately reinstated to the office from which he was suspended and shall be entitled to receive any compensation withheld under the provisions of this subparagraph. For the duration of any suspension under this subparagraph, the Governor shall appoint a replacement judge. Upon a final conviction with no appeal or review pending, the office shall be declared vacant and a successor to that office shall be chosen as provided in this Constitution or the laws enacted in pursuance thereof. The provisions of this subparagraph shall not apply to any conviction rendered prior to January 1, 1987.

Paragraph VIII. Due process; review by Supreme Court
No action shall be taken against a judge except after hearing and in accordance with due process of law. No removal or involuntary retirement shall occur except upon order of the Supreme Court after review.

SECTION VIII. DISTRICT ATTORNEYS

Paragraph I. District attorneys; vacancies; qualifications; compensation; duties; immunity

(a) There shall be a district attorney for each judicial circuit, who shall be elected circuit-wide for a term of four years. The successors of present and subsequent incumbents shall be elected by the electors of their respective circuits at the general election held immediately preceding the expiration of their respective terms. District attorneys shall serve until their successors are duly elected and qualified. Vacancies shall be filled by appointment of the Governor.
(b) No person shall be a district attorney unless such person shall have been an active-status member of the State Bar of Georgia for three years immediately preceding such person's election.

(c) The district attorneys shall receive such compensation and allowances as provided by law and shall be entitled to receive such local supplements to their compensation and allowances as may be provided by law.

(d) It shall be the duty of the district attorney to represent the state in all criminal cases in the superior court of such district attorney's circuit and in all cases appealed from the superior court and the juvenile courts of that circuit to the Supreme Court and the Court of Appeals and to perform such other duties as shall be required by law.

(e) District attorneys shall enjoy immunity from private suit for actions arising from the performance of their duties.

Paragraph II. Discipline, removal, and involuntary retirement of district attorneys. Any district attorney may be disciplined, removed or involuntarily retired as provided by general law.

SECTION IX. GENERAL PROVISIONS

Paragraph I. Administration of the judicial system; uniform court rules; advice and consent of councils

The judicial system shall be administered as provided in this Paragraph. Not more than 24 months after the effective date hereof, and from time to time thereafter by amendment, the Supreme Court shall, with the advice and consent of the council of the affected class or classes of trial courts, by order adopt and publish uniform court rules and record-keeping rules which shall provide for the speedy, efficient, and inexpensive resolution of disputes and prosecutions. Each council shall be comprised of all of the judges of the courts of that class.

Paragraph II. Disposition of cases

The Supreme Court and the Court of Appeals shall dispose of every case at the term for which it is entered on the court's docket for hearing or at the next term.

SECTION X. TRANSITION

Paragraph I. Effect of ratification. On the effective date of this article

(1) Superior courts shall continue as superior courts.
(2) State courts shall continue as state courts.
(3) Probate courts shall continue as probate courts.
(4) Juvenile courts shall continue as juvenile courts.
(5) Municipal courts not otherwise named herein, of whatever name, shall continue as and be denominated municipal courts, except that the City Court of Atlanta shall retain its name. Such municipal courts, county recorder's courts, the Civil Courts of Richmond and Bibb counties, and administrative agencies having quasi-judicial powers shall continue with the same jurisdiction as such courts and agencies have on the effective date of this article until otherwise provided by law.
(6) Justice of the peace courts, small claims courts, and magistrate courts operating on the effective date of this Constitution and the County Court of Echols County shall become and be classified as magistrate courts. The County Court of Baldwin County and the County Court of Putnam County shall become and be classified as state courts, with the same jurisdiction and powers as other state courts.

Paragraph II. Continuation of judges

Each judge holding office on the effective date of this article shall continue in office until the expiration of the term of office, as a judge of the court having the same or similar jurisdiction. Each court not named herein shall cease to exist on such date or at the expiration of the term of the incumbent judge, whichever is later; and its jurisdiction shall automatically pass to the new court of the same or similar jurisdiction, in the absence of which court it shall pass to the superior court.

ARTICLE VII: TAXATION AND FINANCE

SECTION I. POWER OF TAXATION

Paragraph I. Taxation; limitations on grants of tax powers

The state may not suspend or irrevocably give, grant, limit, or restrain the right of taxation and all laws, grants, contracts, and other acts to effect any of these purposes are null and void. Except as otherwise provided in this Constitution, the right of taxation shall always be under the complete control of the state.

Paragraph II. Taxing power limited

(a) The annual levy of state ad valorem taxes on tangible property for all purposes, except for defending the state in an emergency, shall not exceed one-fourth mill on each dollar of the assessed value of the property.

(b) So long as the method of taxation in effect on December 31, 1980, for the taxation of shares of stock of banking corporations and other monied capital coming into competition with such banking corporations continues in effect, such shares and other monied capital may be taxed at an annual rate not exceeding five mills on each dollar of the assessed value of the property.

Paragraph III. Uniformity; classification of property; assessment of agricultural land; utilities

(a) All taxes shall be levied and collected under general laws and for public purposes only. Except as otherwise provided in subparagraphs (b), (c), (d), (e), and (f) of this Paragraph, all taxation shall be uniform upon the same class of subjects within the territorial limits of the authority levying the tax.

(b)(1) Except as otherwise provided in this subparagraph (b), classes of subjects for taxation of property shall consist of tangible property and one or more classes of intangible personal property including money; provided, however, that any taxation of intangible personal property may be repealed by general law without approval in a referendum effective for all taxable years beginning on or after January 1, 1996. (2) Subject to the conditions and limitations specified by law, each of the following types of property may be classified as a separate class of property for ad valorem property tax purposes and different rates, methods, and assessment dates may be provided for such properties:

(A) Trailers.
(B) Mobile homes other than those mobile homes which qualify the owner of the home for a homestead exemption from ad valorem taxation.
(C) Heavy-duty equipment motor vehicles owned by nonresidents and operated in this state. (3) Motor vehicles may be classified as a separate class of property for ad valorem property tax purposes, and such class may be divided into separate subclasses for ad valorem purposes. The General Assembly may provide by general law for the ad valorem taxation of motor vehicles including, but not limited to, providing for different rates, methods, assessment dates, and taxpayer liability for such class and for each of its subclasses and need not provide for uniformity of taxation with other classes of property or between or within its subclasses. The General Assembly may also determine what portion of any ad valorem tax on motor vehicles shall be retained by the state. As used in this subparagraph, the term 'motor vehicles' means all vehicles which are self-propelled.

(d) Tangible real property, but no more than 2,000 acres of any single property owner, which is devoted to bona fide agricultural purposes shall be assessed for ad valorem taxation purposes at 75 percent of the value which other tangible real property is assessed. No property shall be entitled to receive the preferential assessment provided for in this subparagraph if the property which would otherwise receive such assessment would result in any person who has a beneficial interest in such property, including any interest in the nature of stock ownership, receiving the benefit of such preferential assessment as to more than

2,000 acres. No property shall be entitled to receive the preferential assessment provided for in this subparagraph unless the conditions set out below are met:

(1) The property must be owned by:

(A)(i) One or more natural or naturalized citizens;
(ii) An estate of which the devisee or heirs are one or more natural or naturalized citizens; or
(iii) A trust of which the beneficiaries are one or more natural or naturalized citizens; or

(B) A family-owned farm corporation, the controlling interest of which is owned by individuals related to each other within the fourth degree of civil reckoning, or which is owned by an estate of which the devisee or heirs are one or more natural or naturalized citizens, or which is owned by a trust of which the beneficiaries are one or more natural or naturalized citizens, and such corporation derived 80 percent or more of its gross income from bona fide agricultural pursuits within this state within the year immediately preceding the year in which eligibility is sought.

(2) The General Assembly shall provide by law:

(A) For a definition of the term 'bona fide agricultural purposes,' but such term shall include timber production;
(B) For additional minimum conditions of eligibility which such properties must meet in order to qualify for the preferential assessment provided for herein, including, but not limited to, the requirement that the owner be required to enter into a covenant with the appropriate taxing authorities to maintain the use of the properties in bona fide agricultural purposes for a period of not less than ten years and for appropriate penalties for the breach of any such covenant.

(3) In addition to the specific conditions set forth in this subparagraph

(c), the General Assembly may place further restrictions upon, but may not relax, the conditions of eligibility for the preferential assessment provided for herein.

(d)(1) The General Assembly shall be authorized by general law to establish as a separate class of property for ad valorem tax purposes any tangible real property which is listed in the National Register of Historic Places or in a state historic register authorized by general law. For such purposes, the General Assembly is authorized by general law to establish a program by which certain properties within such class may be assessed for taxes at different rates or valuations in order to encourage the preservation of such historic properties and to assist in the revitalization of historic areas.

(2) The General Assembly shall be authorized by general law to establish as a separate class of property for ad valorem tax purposes any tangible real property on which there have been releases of hazardous waste, constituents, or substances into the environment. For such purposes, the General Assembly is authorized by general law to establish a program by which certain properties within such class may be assessed for taxes at different rates or valuations in order to encourage the cleanup, reuse, and redevelopment of such properties and to assist in the revitalization thereof by encouraging remedial action.

(e) The General Assembly shall provide by general law:
(1) For the definition and methods of assessment and taxation, such methods to include a formula based on current use, annual productivity, and real property sales data, of: 'bona fide conservation use property' to include bona fide agricultural and timber land not to exceed 2,000 acres of a single owner; and 'bona fide residential transitional property,' to include private single-family residential owner occupied property located in transitional developing areas not to exceed five acres of any single owner. Such methods of assessment and taxation shall be subject to the following conditions:

(A) A property owner desiring the benefit of such methods of assessment and taxation shall be required to enter into a covenant to continue the property in bona fide conservation use or bona fide residential transitional use; and
(B) A breach of such covenant within ten years shall result in a recapture of the tax savings resulting from such methods of assessment and taxation and may result in other appropriate penalties;

(2) That standing timber shall be assessed only once, and such assessment shall be made following its harvest or sale and on the basis of its fair market value at the time of harvest or sale. Said assessment shall be two and one-half times the assessed percentage of value fixed by law for other real property taxed under the uniformity provisions of subparagraph (a) of this Paragraph but in no event greater than its fair market value; and for a method of temporary supplementation of the property tax digest of any county if the implementation of this method of taxing timber reduces the tax digest by more than 20 percent, such supplemental assessed value to be assigned to the properties otherwise benefiting from such method of taxing timber.

(f)(1) The General Assembly shall provide by general law for the definition and methods of assessment and taxation, such methods to include a formula based on current use, annual productivity, and real property sales data, of 'forest land conservation use property' to include only forest land each tract of which exceeds 200 acres of a qualified owner. Such methods of assessment and taxation shall be subject to the following conditions:

(A) A qualified owner shall consist of any individual or individuals or any entity registered to do business in this state;
(B) A qualified owner desiring the benefit of such methods of assessment and taxation shall be required to enter into a covenant to continue the property in forest land use;

(C) All contiguous forest land conservation use property of an owner within a county for which forest land conservation use assessment is sought under this subparagraph shall be in a single covenant;
(D) A breach of such covenant within 15 years shall result in a recapture of the tax savings resulting from such methods of assessment and taxation and may result in other appropriate penalties; and
(E) The General Assembly may provide by general law for a limited exception to the 200 acre requirement in the case of a transfer of ownership of all or a part of the forest land conservation use property during a covenant period to another owner qualified to enter into an original forest land conservation use covenant if the original covenant is continued by both such acquiring owner and the transferor for the remainder of the term, in which event no breach of the covenant shall be deemed to have occurred even if the total size of a tract from which the transfer was made is reduced below 200 acres.

(2) No portion of an otherwise eligible tract of forest land conservation use property shall be entitled to receive simultaneously special assessment and taxation under this subparagraph and either subparagraph (c) or (e) of this Paragraph.
(3)(A) The General Assembly shall appropriate an amount for assistance grants to counties, municipalities, and county and independent school districts to offset revenue loss attributable to the implementation of this subparagraph. Such grants shall be made in such manner and shall be subject to such procedures as may be specified by general law.
(B) If the forest land conservation use property is located in a county, municipality, or county or independent school district where forest land conservation use value causes an ad valorem tax revenue reduction of 3 percent or less due to the implementation of this subparagraph, in each taxable year in which such reduction occurs, the assistance grants to the county, each municipality located therein, and the county or independent school districts located therein shall be in an amount equal to 50

percent of the amount of such reduction.

(C) If the forest land conservation use property is located in a county, municipality, or county or independent school district where forest land conservation use value causes an ad valorem tax revenue reduction of more than 3 percent due to the implementation of this subparagraph, in each taxable year in which such reduction occurs, the assistance grants to the county, each municipality located therein, and the county or independent school districts located therein shall be as follows:

(i) For the first 3 percent of such reduction amount, in an amount equal to 50 percent of the amount of such reduction; and

(ii) For the remainder of such reduction amount, in an amount equal to 100 percent of the amount of such remaining reduction amount.

(4) Such revenue reduction shall be calculated by utilizing forest land fair market value. For purposes of this subparagraph, forest land fair market value means the 2008 fair market value of the forest land. Such 2008 valuation may increase from one taxable year to the next by a rate equal to the percentage change in the price index for gross output of state and local government from the prior year to the current year as defined by the National Income and Product Accounts and determined by the United States Bureau of Economic Analysis and indicated by the Price Index for Government Consumption Expenditures and General Government Gross Output (Table 3.10.4). Such revenue reduction shall be determined by subtracting the aggregate forest land conservation use value of qualified properties from the aggregate forest land fair market value of qualified properties for the applicable tax year and the resulting amount shall be multiplied by the millage rate of the county, municipality, or county or independent school district.

(5) For purposes of this subparagraph, the forest land conservation use value shall not include the value of the standing timber located on forest land conservation use property. (g) The General Assembly may provide for a different method and time of returns, assessments, payment, and collection of ad valorem taxes of public utilities, but not on a greater assessed percentage of value or at a higher rate of taxation than other properties, except that property provided for in subparagraph (c), (d), (e), or (f) of this Paragraph.

SECTION II. EXEMPTIONS FROM AD VALOREM TAXATION

Paragraph I. Unauthorized tax exemptions void
Except as authorized in or pursuant to this Constitution, all laws exempting property from ad valorem taxation are void.

Paragraph II. Exemptions from taxation of property

(a) (1) Except as otherwise provided in this Constitution, no property shall be exempted from ad valorem taxation unless the exemption is approved by two-thirds of the members elected to each branch of the General Assembly in a roll-call vote and by a majority of the qualified electors of the state voting in a referendum thereon.
(2) Homestead exemptions from ad valorem taxation levied by local taxing jurisdictions may be granted by local law conditioned upon approval by a majority of the qualified electors residing within the limits of the local taxing jurisdiction voting in a referendum thereon.
(3) Laws subject to the requirement of a referendum as provided in this subparagraph (a) may originate in either the Senate or the House of Representatives.
(4) The requirements of this subparagraph

(a) shall not apply with respect to a law which codifies or recodifies an exemption previously authorized in the Constitution of 1976 or an exemption authorized pursuant to this Constitution.
(b) The grant of any exemption from ad valorem taxation shall be subject to the conditions, limitations, and administrative procedures specified by law.

Paragraph III. Exemptions which may be authorized locally

(a) (1) The governing authority of any county or municipality, subject to the approval of a majority of the qualified electors of such political subdivision voting in a referendum thereon, may exempt from ad valorem taxation, including all such taxation levied for educational purposes and for state purposes, inventories of goods in the process of manufacture or production, and inventories of finished goods.
(2) Exemptions granted pursuant to this subparagraph (a) may only be revoked by a referendum election called and conducted as provided by law. The call for such referendum shall not be issued within five years from the date such exemptions were first granted and, if the results of the election are in favor of the revocation of such exemptions, then such revocation shall be effective only at the end of a five-year period from the date of such referendum.
(3) The implementation, administration, and revocation of the exemptions authorized in this subparagraph

(a) shall be provided for by law. Until otherwise provided by law, the grant of the exemption shall be subject to the same conditions, limitations, definitions, and procedures provided for the grant of such exemption in the Constitution of 1976 on June 30, 1983.
(b) Repealed.

Paragraph IV. Current property tax exemptions preserved

Those types of exemptions from ad valorem taxation provided for by law on June 30, 1983, are hereby continued in effect as statutory law until otherwise provided for by law. Any law which reduces or repeals any homestead exemption in existence on June 30, 1983, or created thereafter must be approved by two-thirds of the members elected to each branch of the General Assembly in a roll-call vote and by a majority of the qualified electors of the state or the affected local taxing jurisdiction voting in a referendum thereon. Any law which reduces or repeals exemptions granted to religious or burial grounds or institutions of purely public charity must be approved by two-thirds of the members elected to each branch of the General Assembly.

Paragraph V. Disabled veteran's homestead exemption
Except as otherwise provided in this paragraph, the amount of the homestead exemption granted to disabled veterans shall be the greater of $32,500.00 or the maximum amount which may be granted to a disabled veteran under Section 802 of Title 38 of the United States Code as hereafter amended. Such exemption shall be granted to: those persons eligible for such exemption on June 30, 1983; to disabled American veterans of any war or armed conflict who are disabled due to loss or loss of use of one lower extremity together with the loss or loss of use of one upper extremity which so affects the functions of balance or propulsion as to preclude locomotion without the aid of braces, crutches, canes, or a wheelchair; and to disabled veterans hereafter becoming eligible for assistance in acquiring housing under Section 801 of the United States Code as hereafter amended. The General Assembly may by general law provide for a different amount or a different method of determining the amount of or eligibility for the homestead exemption granted to disabled veterans. Any such law shall be enacted by a simple majority of the votes of all the members to which each house is entitled and may become effective without referendum. Such law may provide that the amount of or eligibility for the exemption shall be determined by reference to laws enacted by the United States Congress.

SECTION IIA. HOMEOWNER'S INCENTIVE ADJUSTMENT

Paragraph I. State grants; adjustment amount.
For each taxable year, a homeowner's incentive adjustment may be applied to the return of each taxpayer claiming such state-wide homestead exemption as may be specified by general law. The amount of such adjustment may provide a taxpayer with a

benefit equivalent to a homestead exemption of up to $18,000.00 of the assessed value of a taxpayer's homestead or the taxpayer's ad valorem property tax liability on the homestead, whichever is lower. The General Assembly may appropriate such amount each year for grants to local governments and school districts as homeowner tax relief grants. The adjustments and grants authorized by this Paragraph shall be made in such manner and shall be subject to the procedures and conditions as may be specified by general law heretofore or hereafter enacted.

SECTION III. PURPOSES AND METHOD OF STATE TAXATION

Paragraph I. Taxation; purposes for which powers may be exercised

(a) Except as otherwise provided in this Constitution, the power of taxation over the whole state may be exercised for any purpose authorized by law. Any purpose for which the powers of taxation over the whole state could have been exercised on June 30, 1983, shall continue to be a purpose for which such powers may be exercised.
(b) Subject to conditions and limitations as may be provided by law, the power of taxation may be exercised to make grants for tax relief purposes to persons for sales tax paid and not otherwise reimbursed on prescription drugs. Credits or relief provided hereunder may be limited only to such reasonable classifications of taxpayers as may be specified by law.

Paragraph II. Revenue to be paid into general fund

(a) Except as otherwise provided in this Constitution, all revenue collected from taxes, fees, and assessments for state purposes, as authorized by revenue measures enacted by the General Assembly, shall be paid into the general fund of the state treasury.

(b)(1) As authorized by law providing for the promotion of any one or more types of agricultural products, fees, assessments, and other charges collected on the sale or processing of agricultural products need not be paid into the general fund of the state treasury. The uniformity requirement of this article shall be satisfied by the application of the agricultural promotion program upon the affected products.
(2) As used in this subparagraph, 'agricultural products' includes, but is not limited to, registered livestock and livestock products, poultry and poultry products, timber and timber products, fish and seafood, and the products of the farms and forests of this state.

Paragraph III. Grants to counties and municipalities
State funds may be granted to counties and municipalities within the state. The grants authorized by this Paragraph shall be made in such manner and form and subject to the procedures and conditions specified by law. The law providing for any such grant may limit the purposes for which the grant funds may be expended.

Paragraph IV. Increase in state income tax rate prohibited
The General Assembly shall not increase the maximum marginal rate of the state income tax above that in effect on January 1, 2015.

SECTION IV. STATE DEBT

Paragraph I. Purposes for which debt may be incurred. The state may incur

(a) Public debt without limit to repel invasion, suppress insurrection, and defend the state in time of war.
(b) Public debt to supply a temporary deficit in the state treasury in any fiscal year created by a delay in collecting the taxes of that year. Such debt shall not exceed, in the aggregate, 5 percent of the total revenue receipts, less refunds, of the state

treasury in the fiscal year immediately preceding the year in which such debt is incurred. The debt incurred shall be repaid on or before the last day of the fiscal year in which it is incurred out of taxes levied for that fiscal year. No such debt may be incurred in any fiscal year under the provisions of this subparagraph (b) if there is then outstanding unpaid debt from any previous fiscal year which was incurred to supply a temporary deficit in the state treasury.

(c) General obligation debt to acquire, construct, develop, extend, enlarge, or improve land, waters, property, highways, buildings, structures, equipment, or facilities of the state, -46 its agencies, departments, institutions, and of those state authorities which were created and activated prior to November 8, 1960.

(d) General obligation debt to provide educational facilities for county and independent school systems and to provide public library facilities for county and independent school systems, counties, municipalities, and boards of trustees of public libraries or boards of trustees of public library systems, and, when the construction of such educational or library facilities has been completed, the title to such facilities shall be vested in the respective local boards of education, counties, municipalities, or public library boards of trustees for which such facilities were constructed.

(e) General obligation debt in order to make loans to counties, municipal corporations, political subdivisions, local authorities, and other local government entities for water or sewerage facilities or systems or for regional or multijurisdictional solid waste recycling or solid waste facilities or systems. It shall not be necessary for the state or a state authority to hold title to or otherwise be the owner of such facilities or systems. General obligation debt for these purposes may be authorized and incurred for administration and disbursement by a state authority created and activated before, on, or after November 8, 1960.

(f) Guaranteed revenue debt by guaranteeing the payment of revenue obligations issued by an instrumentality of the state if such revenue obligations are issued to finance:

(1) Toll bridges or toll roads.
(2) Land public transportation facilities or systems.
(3) Water facilities or systems.
(4) Sewage facilities or systems.
(5) Loans to, and loan programs for, citizens of the state for educational purposes.
(6) Regional or multijurisdictional solid waste recycling or solid waste facilities or systems.

Paragraph II. State general obligation debt and guaranteed revenue debt; limitations

(a) As used in this Paragraph and Paragraph III of this section, 'annual debt service requirements' means the total principal and interest coming due in any state fiscal year. With regard to any issue of debt incurred wholly or in part on a term basis, 'annual debt service requirements' means an amount equal to the total principal and interest payments required to retire such issue in full divided by the number of years from its issue date to its maturity date.

(b) No debt may be incurred under subparagraphs (c), (d), and (e) of Paragraph I of this section or Paragraph V of this section at any time when the highest aggregate annual debt service requirements for the then current year or any subsequent year for outstanding general obligation debt and guaranteed revenue debt, including the proposed debt, and the highest aggregate annual payments for the then current year or any subsequent fiscal year of the state under all contracts then in force to which the provisions of the second paragraph of Article IX, Section VI, Paragraph I(a) of the Constitution of 1976 are applicable, exceed 10 percent of the total revenue receipts, less refunds of the state treasury in the fiscal year immediately preceding the year in which any such debt is to be incurred.

(c) No debt may be incurred under subparagraphs (c) and (d) of Paragraph I of this section at any time when the term of the debt is in excess of 25 years.

(d) No guaranteed revenue debt may be incurred to finance water or sewage treatment facilities or systems when the highest aggregate annual debt service requirements for the then current year or any subsequent fiscal year of the state for outstanding or proposed guaranteed revenue debt for water facilities or systems or sewage facilities or systems exceed 1 percent of the total revenue receipts less refunds, of the state treasury in the fiscal year immediately preceding the year in which any such debt is to be incurred.

(e) The aggregate amount of guaranteed revenue debt incurred to make loans for educational purposes that may be outstanding at any time shall not exceed $18 million, and the aggregate amount of guaranteed revenue debt incurred to purchase, or to lend or deposit against the security of, loans for educational purposes that may be outstanding at any time shall not exceed $72 million.

Paragraph III. State general obligation debt and guaranteed revenue debt; conditions upon issuance; sinking funds and reserve funds

(a) (1) General obligation debt may not be incurred until legislation is enacted stating the purposes, in general or specific terms, for which such issue of debt is to be incurred, specifying the maximum principal amount of such issue and appropriating an amount at least sufficient to pay the highest annual debt service requirements for such issue. All such appropriations for debt service purposes shall not lapse for any reason and shall continue in effect until the debt for which such appropriation was authorized shall have been incurred, but the General Assembly may repeal any such appropriation at any time prior to the incurring of such debt. The General Assembly shall raise by taxation and appropriate each fiscal year, in addition to the sum necessary to make all payments required under contracts entitled to the protection of the second paragraph of Paragraph I(a), Section VI, Article IX of the Constitution of 1976, such amounts as are necessary to pay debt service requirements in such fiscal year on all general obligation debt.

(2)(A) The General Assembly shall appropriate to a special trust fund to be designated 'State of Georgia General Obligation Debt Sinking Fund' such amounts as are necessary to pay annual debt service requirements on all general obligation debt. The sinking fund shall be used solely for the retirement of general obligation debt payable from the fund. If for any reason the monies in the sinking fund are insufficient to make, when due, all payments required with respect to such general obligation debt, the first revenues thereafter received in the general fund of the state shall be set aside by the appropriate state fiscal officer to the extent necessary to cure the deficiency and shall be deposited by the fiscal officer into the sinking fund. The appropriate state fiscal officer may be required to set aside and apply such revenues at the suit of any holder of any general obligation debt incurred under this section.

(B) The obligation to make sinking fund deposits as provided in subparagraph (2)(A) shall be subordinate to the obligation imposed upon the fiscal officers of the state pursuant to the provisions of the second paragraph of Paragraph I(a) of Section VI of Article IX of the Constitution of 1976.

(b)(1) Guaranteed revenue debt may not be incurred until legislation has been enacted authorizing the guarantee of the specific issue of revenue obligations then proposed, reciting that the General Assembly has determined such obligations will be self-liquidating over the life of the issue (which determination shall be conclusive), specifying the maximum principal amount of such issue and appropriating an amount at least equal to the highest annual debt service requirements for such issue.

(2)(A) Each appropriation made for the purposes of subparagraph (b)(1) shall be paid upon the issuance of said obligations into a special trust fund to be designated 'State of Georgia Guaranteed Revenue Debt Common Reserve Fund' to be held together with all other sums similarly appropriated as a common reserve for any payments which may be required by virtue of any guarantee entered into in connection with any issue of guaranteed revenue obligations. No appropriations for the benefit of guaranteed revenue debt shall lapse unless repealed prior to the payment of the appropriation into the common reserve fund.

(B) If any payments are required to be made from the common reserve fund to meet debt service requirements on guaranteed revenue obligations by virtue of an insufficiency of revenues, the amount necessary to cure the deficiency shall be paid from the common reserve fund by the appropriate state fiscal officer. Upon any such payment, the common reserve fund shall be reimbursed from the general funds of the state within ten days following the commencement of any fiscal year of the state for any amounts so paid; provided, however, the obligation to make any such reimbursements shall be subordinate to the obligation imposed upon the fiscal officers of the state pursuant to the second paragraph of Paragraph I(a) of Section VI, Article -48 IX of the Constitution of 1976 and shall also be subordinate to the obligation to make sinking fund deposits for the benefit of general obligation debt. The appropriate state fiscal officer may be required to apply such funds as provided in this subparagraph (b)(2)(B) at the suit of any holder of any such guaranteed revenue obligations.

(C) The amount to the credit of the common reserve fund shall at all times be at least equal to the aggregate highest annual debt service requirements on all outstanding guaranteed revenue obligations entitled to the benefit of the fund. If at the end of any fiscal year of the state the fund is in excess of the required amount, the appropriate state fiscal officer, as designated by law, shall transfer the excess amount to the general funds of the state free of said trust.

(c) The funds in the general obligation debt sinking fund and the guaranteed revenue debt common reserve fund shall be as fully invested as is practicable, consistent with the requirements to make current principal and interest payments. Any such investments shall be restricted to obligations constituting direct and general obligations of the United States government or obligations unconditionally guaranteed as to the payment of principal and interest by the United States government, maturing no longer than 12 months from date of purchase.

Paragraph IV. Certain contracts prohibited
The state, and all state institutions, departments and agencies of the state are prohibited from entering into any contract, except contracts pertaining to guaranteed revenue debt, with any public agency, public corporation, authority, or similar entity if such contract is intended to constitute security for bonds or other obligations issued by any such public agency, public corporation, or authority and, in the event any contract between the state, or any state institution, department or agency of the state and any public agency, public corporation, authority or similar entity, or any revenues from any such contract, is pledged or assigned as security for the repayment of bonds or other obligations, then and in either such event, the appropriation or expenditure of any funds of the state for the payment of obligations under any such contract shall likewise be prohibited.

Paragraph V. Refunding of debt
The state may incur general obligation debt or guaranteed revenue debt to fund or refund any such debt or to fund or refund any obligations issued upon the security of contracts to which the provisions of the second paragraph of Paragraph I(a), Section VI, Article IX of the Constitution of 1976 are applicable. The issuance of any such debt for the purposes of said funding or refunding shall be subject to the 10 percent limitation in Paragraph II(b) of this section to the same extent as debt incurred under Paragraph I of this section; provided, however, in making such computation the annual debt service requirements and annual contract payments remaining on the debt or obligations being funded or refunded shall not be taken into account. The issuance of such debt may be accomplished by resolution of the Georgia State Financing and Investment Commission without any action on the part of the General Assembly and any appropriation made or required to be made with respect to the debt or obligation being funded or refunded shall immediately attach and inure to the benefit of the obligations to be issued in connection with such funding or refunding. Debt incurred in connection with any such funding or refunding shall be the same as that originally authorized by the

General Assembly, except that general obligation debt may be incurred to fund or refund obligations issued upon the security of contracts to which the provisions of the second paragraph of Paragraph I(a), Section VI, Article IX of the Constitution of 1976 are applicable and the continuing appropriations required to be made under this Constitution shall immediately attach and inure to the benefit of the obligation to be issued in connection with such funding or refunding with the same force and effect as though said obligations so funded or refunded had originally been issued as a general obligation debt authorized hereunder. The term of a funding or refunding issue pursuant to this Paragraph shall not extend beyond the term of the original debt or obligation and the total interest on the funding or refunding issue shall not exceed the total interest to be paid on such original debt or obligation. The principal amount of any debt issued in connection with such funding or refunding may exceed the principal amount being funded or refunded to the extent necessary to provide for the payment of any premium thereby incurred.

Paragraph VI. Faith and credit of state pledged debt may be validated

The full faith, credit, and taxing power of the state are hereby pledged to the payment of all public debt incurred under this article and all such debt and the interest on the debt shall be exempt from taxation. Such debt may be validated by judicial proceedings in the manner provided by law. Such validation shall be incontestable and conclusive.

Paragraph VII. Georgia State Financing and Investment Commission; duties

(a) There shall be a Georgia State Financing and Investment Commission. The commission shall consist of the Governor, the President of the Senate, the Speaker of the House of Representatives, the State Auditor, the Attorney General, the director, Fiscal Division, Department of Administrative Services, or such other officer as may be designated by law, and the

Commissioner of Agriculture. The commission shall be responsible for the issuance of all public debt and for the proper application, as provided by law, of the proceeds of such debt to the purposes for which it is incurred; provided, however, the proceeds from guaranteed revenue obligations shall be paid to the issuer thereof and such proceeds and the application thereof shall be the responsibility of such issuer. Debt to be incurred at the same time for more than one purpose may be combined in one issue without stating the purpose separately but the proceeds thereof must be allocated, disbursed and used solely in accordance with the original purpose and without exceeding the principal amount authorized for each purpose set forth in the authorization of the General Assembly and to the extent not so used shall be used to purchase and retire public debt. The commission shall be responsible for the investment of all proceeds to be administered by it and, as provided by law, the income earned on any such investments may be used to pay operating expenses of the commission or placed in a common debt retirement fund and used to purchase and retire any public debt, or any bonds or obligations issued by any public agency, public corporation or authority which are secured by a contract to which the provisions of the second paragraph of Paragraph I(a) of Section VI, Article IX of the Constitution of 1976 are applicable. The commission shall have such additional responsibilities, powers, and duties as are provided by law.

(b) Notwithstanding subparagraph (a) of this Paragraph, proceeds from general obligation debt issued for making loans to local government entities for water or sewerage facilities or systems or for regional or multijurisdictional solid waste recycling or solid waste facilities or systems as provided in Paragraph I(e) of this section shall be paid or transferred to and administered and invested by the unit of state government or state authority made responsible by law for such activities, and the proceeds and investment earnings thereof shall be applied and disbursed by such unit or authority.

Paragraph VIII. State aid forbidden
Except as provided in this Constitution, the credit of the state shall not be pledged or loaned to any individual, company, corporation, or association. The state shall not become a joint owner or stockholder in or with any individual, company, association, or corporation.

Paragraph IX. Construction
Paragraphs I through VIII of this section are for the purpose of providing an effective method of financing the state's needs and their provisions and any law now or hereafter enacted by the General Assembly in furtherance of their provisions shall be liberally construed to effect such purpose. Insofar as any such provisions or any such law may be inconsistent with any other provisions of this Constitution or of any other law, the provisions of such Paragraphs and laws enacted in furtherance of such Paragraphs shall be controlling; provided, however, the provisions of such Paragraphs shall not be so broadly construed as to cause the same to be unconstitutional and in connection with any such construction such Paragraphs shall be deemed to contain such implied limitations as shall be required to accomplish the foregoing.

Paragraph X. Assumption of debts forbidden; exceptions
The state shall not assume the debt, or any part thereof, of any county, municipality, or other political subdivision of the state, unless such debt be contracted to enable the state to repel invasion, suppress civil disorders or insurrection, or defend itself in time of war.

Paragraph XI. Section not to unlawfully impair contracts or revive obligations previously voided

The provisions of this section shall not be construed so as to:

(a) Unlawfully impair the obligation of any contract in effect on June 30, 1983.

(b) Revive or permit the revival of the obligation of any bond or security declared to be void by the Constitution of 1976 or any previous Constitution of this state.

Paragraph XII. Multiyear contracts for energy efficiency or conservation improvement

The General Assembly may by general law authorize state governmental entities to incur debt for the purpose of entering into multiyear contracts for governmental energy efficiency or conservation improvement projects in which payments are guaranteed over the term of the contract by vendors based on the realization of specified savings or revenue gains attributable solely to the improvements; provided, however, that any such contract shall not exceed ten years unless otherwise provided by general law.

Paragraph XIII. Multiyear rental agreements

The General Assembly may by general law authorize the State Properties Commission, the Board of Regents of the University System of Georgia, and the Georgia Department of Labor to enter into rental agreements for the possession and use of real property without obligating present funds for the full amount of obligation the state may bear under the full term of any such rental agreement. Any such agreement shall provide for the termination of the agreement in the event of insufficient funds.

ARTICLE VIII: EDUCATION

SECTION I. PUBLIC EDUCATION

Paragraph I. Public education; free public education prior to college or postsecondary level; support by taxation.

The provision of an adequate public education for the citizens shall be a primary obligation of the State of Georgia. Public education for the citizens prior to the college or postsecondary level shall be free and shall be provided for by taxation, and the General Assembly may by general law provide for the establishment of education policies for such public education. The expense of other public education shall be provided for in such manner and in such amount as may be provided by law.

SECTION II. STATE BOARD OF EDUCATION

Paragraph I. State Board of Education

(a) There shall be a State Board of Education which shall consist of one member from each congressional district in the state appointed by the Governor and confirmed by the Senate. The Governor shall not be a member of said board. The ten members in office on June 30, 1983, shall serve out the remainder of their respective terms. As each term of office expires, the Governor shall appoint a successor as herein provided. The terms of office of all members appointed after the effective date of this Constitution shall be for seven years. Members shall serve until their successors are appointed and qualified. In the event of a vacancy on the board by death, resignation, removal, or any reason other than expiration of a member's term, the Governor shall fill such vacancy; and the person so appointed shall serve until confirmed by the Senate and, upon confirmation, shall serve for the unexpired term of office.
(b) The State Board of Education shall have such powers and duties as provided by law.
(c) The State Board of Education may accept bequests, donations, grants, and transfers of land, buildings, and other

property for the use of the state educational system.

(d) The qualifications, compensation, and removal from office of the members of the board of education shall be as provided by law.

SECTION III. STATE SCHOOL SUPERINTENDENT

Paragraph I. State School Superintendent
There shall be a State School Superintendent, who shall be the executive officer of the State Board of Education, elected at the same time and in the same manner and for the same term as that of the Governor. The State School Superintendent shall have such qualifications and shall be paid such compensation as may be fixed by law. No member of the State Board of Education shall be eligible for election as State School Superintendent during the time for which such member shall have been appointed.

SECTION IV. BOARD OF REGENTS
Paragraph I. University System of Georgia; board of regents

(a) There shall be a Board of Regents of the University System of Georgia which shall consist of one member from each congressional district in the state and five additional members from the state at large, appointed by the Governor and confirmed by the Senate. The Governor shall not be a member of said board. The members in office on June 30, 1983, shall serve out the remainder of their respective terms. As each term of office expires, the Governor shall appoint a successor as herein provided. All such terms of members shall be for seven years. Members shall serve until their successors are appointed and qualified. In the event of a vacancy on the board by death, resignation, removal, or any reason other than the expiration of a member's term, the Governor shall fill such vacancy; and the person so appointed shall serve until confirmed by the Senate and, upon confirmation, shall serve for the unexpired term of office.

(b) The board of regents shall have the exclusive authority to create new public colleges, junior colleges, and universities in the State of Georgia, subject to approval by majority vote in the House of Representatives and the Senate. Such vote shall not be required to change the status of a college, institution or university existing on the effective date of this Constitution. The government, control, and management of the University System of Georgia and all of the institutions in said system shall be vested in the Board of Regents of the University System of Georgia.

(c) All appropriations made for the use of any or all institutions in the university system shall be paid to the board of regents in a lump sum, with the power and authority in said board to allocate and distribute the same among the institutions under its control in such way and manner and in such amounts as will further an efficient and economical administration of the university system.

(d) The board of regents may hold, purchase, lease, sell, convey, or otherwise dispose of public property, execute conveyances thereon, and utilize the proceeds arising therefrom; may exercise the power of eminent domain in the manner provided by law; and shall have such other powers and duties as provided by law.

(e) The board of regents may accept bequests, donations, grants, and transfers of land, buildings, and other property for the use of the University System of Georgia.

(f) The qualifications, compensation, and removal from office of the members of the board of regents shall be as provided by law.

SECTION V. LOCAL SCHOOL SYSTEMS

Paragraph I. School systems continued; consolidation of school systems authorized; new independent school systems prohibited

Authority is granted to county and area boards of education to establish and maintain public schools within their limits; provided, however, that the authority provided for in this paragraph shall not diminish any authority of the General Assembly otherwise granted under this article, including the authority to establish special schools as provided for in Article VIII, Section V, Paragraph VII. Existing county and independent school systems shall be continued, except that the General Assembly may provide by law for the consolidation of two or more county school systems, independent school systems, portions thereof, or any combination thereof into a single county or area school system under the control and management of a county or area board of education, under such terms and conditions as the General Assembly may prescribe; but no such consolidation shall become effective until approved by a majority of the qualified voters voting thereon in each separate school system proposed to be consolidated. No independent school system shall hereafter be established.

Paragraph II. Boards of education
Each school system shall be under the management and control of a board of education, the members of which shall be elected as provided by law. School board members shall reside within the territory embraced by the school system and shall have such compensation and additional qualifications as may be provided by law. Any board of education to which the members are appointed as of December 31, 1992, shall continue as an appointed board of education through December 31, 1993, and the appointed members of such board of education who are in office on December 31, 1992, shall continue in office as members of such appointed board until December 31, 1993, on which date the terms of office of all appointed members shall end.

Paragraph III. School superintendents
There shall be a school superintendent of each system appointed by the board of education who shall be the executive officer of the board of education and shall have such qualifications, powers, and duties as provided by general law. Any elected school superintendent in office on January 1, 1993, shall continue to serve out the remainder of his or her respective term of office and shall be replaced by an appointee of the board of education at the expiration of such term.

Paragraph IV. Reserved

Paragraph V. Power of boards to contract with each other

(a) Any two or more boards of education may contract with each other for the care, education, and transportation of pupils and for such other activities as they may be authorized by law to perform.
(b) The General Assembly may provide by law for the sharing of facilities or services by and between local boards of education under such joint administrative authority as may be authorized.
Paragraph VI. Power of boards to accept bequests, donations, grants, and transfers. The board of education of each school system may accept bequests, donations, grants, and transfers of land, buildings, and other property for the use of such system.

Paragraph VII. Special schools

(a) The General Assembly may provide by law for the creation of special schools in such areas as may require them and may provide for the participation of local boards of education in the establishment of such schools under such terms and conditions as it may provide; but no bonded indebtedness may be incurred nor a school tax levied for the support of special schools without the approval of the local board of education and a majority of the qualified voters voting thereon in each of the systems affected. Any special schools shall be operated in conformity with regulations of the State Board of Education pursuant to provisions of law. Special schools may include state charter schools; provided, however, that special schools shall only be public schools. A state charter school under this section shall mean a public school that operates under the terms of a charter between the State Board of Education and a charter petitioner; provided, however, that such state charter schools shall not include private, sectarian, religious, or for profit schools or private educational institutions; provided, further, that this Paragraph shall not be construed to prohibit a local board of education from establishing a local charter school pursuant to Article VIII, Section V, Paragraph I. The state is authorized to expend state funds for the support and maintenance of special schools in such amount and manner as may be provided by law; provided, however, no deduction shall be made to any state funding which a local school system is otherwise authorized to receive pursuant to general law as a direct result or consequence of the enrollment in a state charter school of a specific student or students who reside within the geographic boundaries of the local school system.

(b) Nothing contained herein shall be construed to affect the authority of local boards of education or of the state to support and maintain special schools created prior to June 30, 1983.

SECTION VI. LOCAL TAXATION FOR EDUCATION

Paragraph I. Local taxation for education

(a) The board of education of each school system shall annually certify to its fiscal authority or authorities a school tax not greater than 20 mills per dollar for the support and maintenance of education. Said fiscal authority or authorities shall annually levy said tax upon the assessed value of all taxable property within the territory served by said school system, provided that the levy made by an area board of education, which levy shall not be greater than 20 mills per dollar, shall be in such amount and within such limits as may be prescribed by local law applicable thereto. (b) School tax funds shall be expended only for the support and maintenance of public schools, public vocational-technical schools, public education, and activities necessary or incidental thereto, including school lunch purposes.

(c) The 20 mill limitation provided for in subparagraph (a) of this Paragraph shall not apply to those school systems which are authorized on June 30, 1983, to levy a school tax in excess thereof.

(d) The method of certification and levy of the school tax provided for in subparagraph (a) of this Paragraph shall not apply to those systems that are authorized on June 30, 1983, to utilize a different method of certification and levy of such tax; but the General Assembly may by law require that such systems be brought into conformity with the method of certification and levy herein provided.

Paragraph II. Increasing or removing tax rate
The mill limitation in effect on June 30, 1983, for any school system may be increased or removed by action of the respective boards of education, but only after such action has been approved by a majority of the qualified voters voting thereon in the particular school system to be affected in the manner provided by law.

Paragraph III. School tax collection reimbursement
The General Assembly may by general law require local boards of education to reimburse the appropriate governing authority for the collection of school taxes, provided that any rate established may be reduced by local act.

Paragraph IV. Sales tax for educational purposes

(a) The board of education of each school district in a county in which no independent school district is located may by resolution and the board of education of each county school district and the board of education of each independent school district located within such county may by concurrent resolutions impose, levy, and collect a sales and use tax for educational purposes of such school districts conditioned upon approval by a majority of the qualified voters residing within the limits of the local taxing jurisdiction voting in a referendum thereon. This tax shall be at the rate of 1 percent and shall be imposed for a period of time not to exceed five years, but in all other respects, except as otherwise provided in this Paragraph, shall correspond to and be levied in the same manner as the tax provided for by Article 3 of Chapter 8 of Title 48 of the Official Code of Georgia Annotated, relating to the special county 1 percent sales and use tax, as now or hereafter amended. Proceedings for the reimposition of such tax shall be in the same manner as proceedings for the initial imposition of the tax, but the newly authorized tax shall not be imposed until the expiration of the tax then in effect.

(b) The purpose or purposes for which the proceeds of the tax are to be used and may be expended include:

(1) Capital outlay projects for educational purposes;

(2) The retirement of previously incurred general obligation debt with respect only to capital outlay projects of the school system; provided, however, that the tax authorized under this Paragraph shall only be expended for the purpose authorized under this subparagraph (b)(2) if all ad valorem property taxes levied or scheduled to be levied prior to the maturity of any such then outstanding general obligation debt to be retired by the proceeds of the tax imposed under this Paragraph shall be reduced by a total amount equal to the total amount of proceeds of the tax imposed under this Paragraph to be applied to retire such bonded indebtedness. In the event of failure to comply with the requirements of this subparagraph (b)(2), as certified by the Department of Revenue, no further funds shall be expended under this subparagraph (b)(2) by such county or independent board of education and all such funds shall be maintained in a separate, restricted account and held solely for the expenditure for future capital outlay projects for educational purposes; or

(3) A combination of the foregoing.

(c) The resolution calling for the imposition of the tax and the ballot question shall each describe:

(1) The specific capital outlay projects to be funded, or the specific debt to be retired, or both, if applicable;

(2) The maximum cost of such project or projects and, if applicable, the maximum amount of debt to be retired, which cost and amount of debt shall also be the maximum amount of net proceeds to be raised by the tax; and

(3) The maximum period of time, to be stated in calendar years or calendar quarters and not to exceed five years.

(d) Nothing in this Paragraph shall prohibit a county and those municipalities located in such county from imposing as additional taxes local sales and use taxes authorized by general law.

(e) The tax imposed pursuant to this Paragraph shall not be subject to and shall not count with respect to any general law limitation regarding the maximum amount of local sales and use taxes which may be levied in any jurisdiction in this state.

(f) The tax imposed pursuant to this Paragraph shall not be subject to any sales and use tax exemption with respect to the sale or use of food and beverages which is imposed by law.

(g) The net proceeds of the tax shall be distributed between the county school district and the independent school districts, or portion thereof, located in such county according to the ratio the student enrollment in each school district, or portion thereof, bears to the total student enrollment of all school districts in the county or upon such other formula for distribution as may be authorized by local law. For purposes of this subparagraph, student enrollment shall be based on the latest FTE count prior to the referendum on imposing the tax.

(h) Excess proceeds of the tax which remain following expenditure of proceeds for authorized projects or purposes for education shall be used solely for the purpose of reducing any indebtedness of the school system. In the event there is no indebtedness, such excess proceeds shall be used by such school system for the purpose of reducing its millage rate in an amount equivalent to the amount of such excess proceeds.

(i) The tax authorized by this Paragraph may be imposed, levied, and collected as provided in this Paragraph without further action by the General Assembly, but the General Assembly shall be authorized by general law to further define and implement its provisions including, but not limited to, the authority to specify the percentage of net proceeds to be allocated among the projects and purposes for which the tax was levied. (j)(1) Notwithstanding any provision of any constitutional amendment continued in force and effect pursuant to Article XI, Section I, Paragraph IV(a) and except as otherwise provided in subparagraph (j)(2) of this Paragraph, any political subdivision whose ad valorem taxing powers are restricted pursuant to such a constitutional amendment may receive the proceeds of the tax authorized under this Paragraph or of any local sales and use tax authorized by general law, or any combination of such taxes, without any corresponding limitation of its ad valorem taxing powers which would otherwise be required under such constitutional amendment.

(2) The restriction on and limitation of ad valorem taxing powers described in subparagraph (j)(1) of this Paragraph shall remain applicable with respect to proceeds received from the levy of a local sales and use tax specifically authorized by a constitutional amendment in force and effect pursuant to Article XI, Section I, Paragraph IV(a), as opposed to a local sales and use tax authorized by this Paragraph or by general law.

SECTION VII. EDUCATIONAL ASSISTANCE

Paragraph I. Educational assistance programs authorized

(a) Pursuant to laws now or hereafter enacted by the General Assembly, public funds may be expended for any of the following purposes:

(1) To provide grants, scholarships, loans, or other assistance to students and to parents of students for educational purposes.
(2) To provide for a program of guaranteed loans to students and to parents of students for educational purposes and to pay interest, interest subsidies, and fees to lenders on such loans. The General Assembly is authorized to provide such tax exemptions to lenders as shall be deemed advisable in connection with such program.
(3) To match funds now or hereafter available for student assistance pursuant to any federal law.
(4) To provide grants, scholarships, loans, or other assistance to public employees for educational purposes.
(5) To provide for the purchase of loans made to students for educational purposes who have completed a program of study in a field in which critical shortages exist and for cancellation of

repayment of such loans, interest, and charges thereon.

(b) Contributions made in support of any educational assistance program now or hereafter established under provisions of this section may be deductible for state income tax purposes as now or hereafter provided by law.

(c) The General Assembly shall be authorized by general law to provide for an education trust fund to assist students and parents of students in financing postsecondary education and to provide for contracts between the fund and purchasers for the advance payment of tuition by each purchaser for a qualified beneficiary to attend a state institution of higher education. Such general law shall provide for such terms, conditions, and limitations as the General Assembly shall deem necessary for the implementation of this subparagraph. Notwithstanding any provision of this Constitution to the contrary, the General Assembly shall be authorized to provide for the guarantee of such contracts with state revenues.

Paragraph II. Guaranteed revenue debt
Guaranteed revenue debt may be incurred to provide funds to make loans to students and to parents of students for educational purposes, to purchase loans made to students and to parents of students for educational purposes, or to lend or make deposits of such funds with lenders which shall be secured by loans made to students and to parents of students for educational purposes. Any such debt shall be incurred in accordance with the procedures and requirements of Article VII, Section IV of this Constitution.

Paragraph III. Public authorities
Public authorities or public corporations heretofore or hereafter created for such purposes shall be authorized to administer educational assistance programs and, in connection therewith, may exercise such powers as may now or hereafter be provided by law.

Paragraph IV. Waiver of tuition
The Board of Regents of the University System of Georgia shall be authorized to establish programs allowing attendance at units of the University System of Georgia without payment of tuition or other fees, but the General Assembly may provide by law for the establishment of any such program for the benefit of elderly citizens of the state.

ARTICLE IX: COUNTIES AND MUNICIPAL CORPORATIONS

SECTION I. COUNTIES

Paragraph I. Counties a body corporate and politic

Each county shall be a body corporate and politic with such governing authority and with such powers and limitations as are provided in this Constitution and as provided by law. The governing authorities of the several counties shall remain as prescribed by law on June 30, 1983, until otherwise provided by law.

Paragraph II. Number of counties limited; county boundaries and county sites; county consolidation

(a) There shall not be more than 159 counties in this state.
(b) The metes and bounds of the several counties and the county sites shall remain as prescribed by law on June 30, 1983, unless changed under the operation of a general law.
(c) The General Assembly may provide by law for the consolidation of two or more counties into one or the division of a county and the merger of portions thereof into other counties under such terms and conditions as it may prescribe; but no such consolidation, division, or merger shall become effective unless approved by a majority of the qualified voters voting thereon in each of the counties proposed to be consolidated, divided, or merged.

Paragraph III. County officers; election; term; compensation

(a) The clerk of the superior court, judge of the probate court, sheriff, tax receiver, tax collector, and tax commissioner, where such office has replaced the tax receiver and tax collector, shall be elected by the qualified voters of their respective counties for terms of four years and shall have such qualifications, powers, and duties as provided by general law.

(b) County officers listed in subparagraph (a) of this Paragraph may be on a fee basis, salary basis, or fee basis supplemented by salary, in such manner as may be directed by law. Minimum compensation for said county officers may be established by the General Assembly by general law. Such minimum compensation may be supplemented by local law or, if such authority is delegated by local law, by action of the county governing authority.
(c) The General Assembly may consolidate the offices of tax receiver and tax collector into the office of tax commissioner.
Paragraph IV. Civil service systems. The General Assembly may by general law authorize the establishment by county governing authorities of civil service systems covering county employees or covering county employees and employees of the elected county officers.

SECTION II. HOME RULE FOR COUNTIES AND MUNICIPALITIES

Paragraph I. Home rule for counties

(a) The governing authority of each county shall have legislative power to adopt clearly reasonable ordinances, resolutions, or regulations relating to its property, affairs, and local government for which no provision has been made by general law and which is not inconsistent with this Constitution or any local law applicable thereto. Any such local law shall remain in force and effect until amended or repealed as provided in subparagraph (b). This, however, shall not restrict the authority of the General Assembly by general law to further define this power or to broaden, limit, or otherwise regulate the exercise thereof. The General Assembly shall not pass any local law to repeal, modify, or supersede any action taken by a county governing authority under this section except as authorized under subparagraph (c) hereof.
(b) Except as provided in subparagraph (c), a county may, as an incident of its home rule power, amend or repeal the local acts applicable to its governing authority by following either of the

procedures hereinafter set forth:

(1) Such local acts may be amended or repealed by a resolution or ordinance duly adopted at two regular consecutive meetings of the county governing authority not less than seven nor more than 60 days apart. A notice containing a synopsis of the proposed amendment or repeal shall be published in the official county organ once a week for three weeks within a period of 60 days immediately preceding its final adoption. Such notice shall state that a copy of the proposed amendment or repeal is on file in the office of the clerk of the superior court of the county for the purpose of examination and inspection by the public. The clerk of the superior court shall furnish anyone, upon written request, a copy of the proposed amendment or repeal. No amendment or repeal hereunder shall be valid to change or repeal an amendment adopted pursuant to a referendum as provided in (2) of this subparagraph or to change or repeal a local act of the General Assembly ratified in a referendum by the electors of such county unless at least 12 months have elapsed after such referendum. No amendment hereunder shall be valid if inconsistent with any provision of this Constitution or if provision has been made therefor by general law.

(2) Amendments to or repeals of such local acts or ordinances, resolutions, or regulations adopted pursuant to subparagraph (a) hereof may be initiated by a petition filed with the judge of the probate court of the county containing, in cases of counties with a population of 5,000 or less, the signatures of at least 25 percent of the electors registered to vote in the last general election; in cases of counties with a population of more than 5,000 but not more than 50,000, at least 20 percent of the electors registered to vote in the last general election; and, in cases of a county with a population of more than 50,000, at least 10 percent of the electors registered to vote in the last general election, which petition shall specifically set forth the exact language of the proposed amendment or repeal. The judge of the probate court shall determine the validity of such petition within 60 days of its being filed with the judge of the probate court. In the event the judge of the probate court determines that such petition is valid, it shall be his duty to issue the call for an election for the purpose of submitting such amendment or repeal to the registered electors of the county for their approval or rejection. Such call shall be issued not less than ten nor more than 60 days after the date of the filing of the petition. He shall set the date of such election for a day not less than 60 nor more than 90 days after the date of such filing. The judge of the probate court shall cause a notice of the date of said election to be published in the official organ of the county once a week for three weeks immediately preceding such date. Said notice shall also contain a synopsis of the proposed amendment or repeal and shall state that a copy thereof is on file in the office of the judge of the probate court of the county for the purpose of examination and inspection by the public. The judge of the probate court shall furnish anyone, upon written request, a copy of the proposed amendment or repeal. If more than one-half of the votes cast on such question are for approval of the amendment or repeal, it shall become of full force and effect; otherwise, it shall be void and of no force and effect. The expense of such election shall be borne by the county, and it shall be the duty of the judge of the probate court to hold and conduct such election. Such election shall be held under the same laws and rules and regulations as govern special elections, except as otherwise provided herein. It shall be the duty of the judge of the probate court to canvass the returns and declare and certify the result of the election. It shall be his further duty to certify the result thereof to the Secretary of State in accordance with the provisions of subparagraph (g) of this Paragraph. A referendum on any such amendment or repeal shall not be held more often than once each year. No amendment hereunder shall be valid if inconsistent with any provision of this Constitution or if provision has been made therefor by general law. In the event that the judge of the probate court determines that such petition was not valid, he shall cause to be published in explicit detail the reasons why such petition is not valid; provided, however, that, in any proceeding in which the validity of the petition is at issue, the tribunal considering such issue shall not be limited by the reasons assigned. Such publication shall be in the official organ of the county in the week immediately following the date on which such petition is declared to be not valid.

(c) The power granted to counties in subparagraphs (a) and (b) above shall not be construed to extend to the following matters or any other matters which the General Assembly by general law has preempted or may hereafter preempt, but such matters shall be the subject of general law or the subject of local acts of the General Assembly to the extent that the enactment of such local acts is otherwise permitted under this Constitution:

(1) Action affecting any elective county office, the salaries thereof, or the personnel thereof, except the personnel subject to the jurisdiction of the county governing authority.
(2) Action affecting the composition, form, procedure for election or appointment, compensation, and expenses and allowances in the nature of compensation of the county governing authority.
(3) Action defining any criminal offense or providing for criminal punishment.
(4) Action adopting any form of taxation beyond that authorized by law or by this Constitution.
(5) Action extending the power of regulation over any business activity regulated by the Georgia Public Service Commission beyond that authorized by local or general law or by this Constitution.
(6) Action affecting the exercise of the power of eminent domain.
(7) Action affecting any court or the personnel thereof.
(8) Action affecting any public school system.

(d) The power granted in subparagraphs (a) and (b) of this Paragraph shall not include the power to take any action affecting the private or civil law governing private or civil relationships, except as is incident to the exercise of an independent governmental power.
(e) Nothing in subparagraphs (a), (b), (c), or (d) shall affect the

provisions of subparagraph (f) of this Paragraph.

(f) The governing authority of each county is authorized to fix the salary, compensation, and expenses of those employed by such governing authority and to establish and maintain retirement or pension systems, insurance, workers' compensation, and hospitalization benefits for said employees.

(g) No amendment or revision of any local act made pursuant to subparagraph (b) of this section shall become effective until a copy of such amendment or revision, a copy of the required notice of publication, and an affidavit of a duly authorized representative of the newspaper in which such notice was published to the effect that said notice has been published as provided in said subparagraph has been filed with the Secretary of State. The Secretary of State shall provide for the publication and distribution of all such amendments and revisions at least annually.

Paragraph II. Home rule for municipalities

The General Assembly may provide by law for the self-government of municipalities and to that end is expressly given the authority to delegate its power so that matters pertaining to municipalities may be dealt with without the necessity of action by the General Assembly.

Paragraph III. Supplementary powers

(a) In addition to and supplementary of all powers possessed by or conferred upon any county, municipality, or any combination thereof, any county, municipality, or any combination thereof may exercise the following powers and provide the following services:

(1) Police and fire protection.
(2) Garbage and solid waste collection and disposal.
(3) Public health facilities and services, including hospitals, ambulance and emergency rescue services, and animal control.

(4) Street and road construction and maintenance, including curbs, sidewalks, street lights, and devices to control the flow of traffic on streets and roads constructed by counties and municipalities or any combination thereof.
(5) Parks, recreational areas, programs, and facilities.
(6) Storm water and sewage collection and disposal systems.
(7) Development, storage, treatment, purification, and distribution of water.
(8) Public housing.
(9) Public transportation.
(10) Libraries, archives, and arts and sciences programs and facilities.
(11) Terminal and dock facilities and parking facilities.
(12) Codes, including building, housing, plumbing, and electrical codes.
(13) Air quality control.
(14) The power to maintain and modify heretofore existing retirement or pension systems, including such systems heretofore created by general laws of local application by population classification, and to continue in effect or modify other benefits heretofore provided as a part of or in addition to such retirement or pension systems and the power to create and maintain retirement or pension systems for any elected or appointed public officers and employees whose compensation is paid in whole or in part from county or municipal funds and for the beneficiaries of such officers and employees.

(b) Unless otherwise provided by law,

(1) No county may exercise any of the powers listed in subparagraph (a) of this Paragraph or provide any service listed therein inside the boundaries of any municipality or any other county except by contract with the municipality or county affected; and
(2) No municipality may exercise any of the powers listed in subparagraph (a) of this Paragraph or provide any service listed therein outside its own boundaries except by contract with the county or municipality affected.

(c) Nothing contained within this Paragraph shall operate to prohibit the General Assembly from enacting general laws relative to the subject matters listed in subparagraph (a) of this Paragraph or to prohibit the General Assembly by general law from regulating, restricting, or limiting the exercise of the powers listed therein; but it may not withdraw any such powers.

(d) Except as otherwise provided in subparagraph (b) of this Paragraph, the General Assembly shall act upon the subject matters listed in subparagraph (a) of this Paragraph only by general law.

Paragraph IV. Planning and zoning

The governing authority of each county and of each municipality may adopt plans and may exercise the power of zoning. This authorization shall not prohibit the General Assembly from enacting general laws establishing procedures for the exercise of such power.

Paragraph V. Eminent domain.

The governing authority of each county and of each municipality may exercise the power of eminent domain for any public purpose subject to any limitations on the exercise of such power as may be provided by general law. Notwithstanding the provisions of any local amendment to the Constitution continued in effect pursuant to Article XI, Section I, Paragraph IV or any existing general law, each exercise of eminent domain by a nonelected housing or development authority shall be first approved by the elected governing authority of the county or municipality within which the property is located.

Paragraph VI. Special districts

As hereinafter provided in this Paragraph, special districts may be created for the provision of local government services within such districts; and fees, assessments, and taxes may be levied and collected within such districts to pay, wholly or partially, the cost of providing such services therein and to construct and maintain facilities therefor. Such special districts may be created and fees, assessments, or taxes may be levied and collected therein by any one or more of the following methods:

(a) By general law which directly creates the districts.
(b) By general law which requires the creation of districts under conditions specified by such general law.
(c) By municipal or county ordinance or resolution, except that no such ordinance or resolution may supersede a law enacted by the General Assembly pursuant to subparagraphs (a) or (b) of this Paragraph.

Paragraph VII. Community redevelopment

(A) Each condemnation of privately held property for redevelopment purposes must be approved by vote of the elected governing authority of the city within which the property is located, if any, or otherwise by the governing authority of the county within which the property is located. The power of eminent domain shall not be used for redevelopment purposes by any entity, except for public use, as defined by general law.
(a) The General Assembly may authorize any county, municipality, or housing authority to undertake and carry out community redevelopment.
(b) The General Assembly is also authorized to grant to counties or municipalities for redevelopment purposes and in connection with redevelopment programs, as such purposes and programs are defined by general law, the power to issue tax allocation bonds, as defined by such law, and the power to incur other obligations, without either such bonds or obligations constituting debt within the meaning of Section V of this article, and the power to enter into contracts for any period not exceeding 30 years with private persons, firms, corporations, and business entities. Such general law may authorize the use of county, municipal, and school tax funds, or any combination thereof, to fund such redevelopment purposes and programs, including the payment of debt service on tax allocation bonds, notwithstanding Section VI of Article VIII or any other provision of this Constitution and regardless of whether any county, municipality, or local board of education approved the use of such tax funds

for such purposes and programs before January 1, 2009. No county, municipal, or school tax funds may be used for such purposes and programs without the approval by resolution of the applicable governing body of the county, municipality, or local board of education. No school tax funds may be used for such purposes and programs except as authorized by general law after January 1, 2009; provided, however, that any school tax funds pledged for the repayment of tax allocation bonds which have been judicially validated pursuant to general law shall continue to be used for such purposes and programs. Notwithstanding the grant of these powers pursuant to general law, no county or municipality may exercise these powers unless so authorized by local law and unless such powers are exercised in conformity with those terms and conditions for such exercise as established by that local law. The provisions of any such local law shall conform to those requirements established by general law regarding such powers. No such local law, or any amendment thereto, shall become effective unless approved in a referendum by a majority of the qualified voters voting thereon in the county or municipality directly affected by that local law.

(c) The General Assembly is authorized to provide by general law for the creation of enterprise zones by counties or municipalities, or both. Such law may provide for exemptions, credits, or reductions of any tax or taxes levied within such zones by the state, a county, a municipality, or any combination thereof. Such exemptions shall be available only to such persons, firms, or corporations which create job opportunities within the enterprise zone for unemployed, low, and moderate income persons in accordance with the standards set forth in such general law. Such general law shall further define enterprise zones so as to limit such tax exemptions, credits, or reductions to persons and geographic areas which are determined to be underdeveloped as evidenced by the unemployment rate and the average personal income in the area when compared to the remainder of the state. The General Assembly may by general law further define areas qualified for creation of enterprise zones and may provide for all matters relative to the creation, approval, and termination of such zones.

(d) The existence in a community of real property which is maintained in a blighted condition increases the burdens of state and local government by increasing the need for governmental services, including but not limited to social services, public safety services, and code enforcement services. Rehabilitation of blighted property decreases the need for such governmental services. In recognition of such service needs and in order to encourage community redevelopment, the counties and municipalities of this state are authorized to establish community redevelopment tax incentive programs as authorized in this subparagraph. A community redevelopment tax incentive program shall be established by ordinance of the county or municipality. Any such program and ordinance shall include the following elements:

(1) The ordinance shall specify ascertainable standards which shall be applied in determining whether property is maintained in a blighted condition. The ordinance shall provide that property shall not be subject to official identification as maintained in a blighted condition and shall not be subject to increased taxation if the property is a dwelling house which is being used as the primary residence of one or more persons; and
(2) The ordinance shall establish a procedure for the official identification of real property in the county or municipality which is maintained in a blighted condition. Such procedure shall include notice to the property owner and the opportunity for a hearing with respect to such determination.
(3) The ordinance shall specify an increased rate of ad valorem taxation to be applied to property which has been officially identified as maintained in a blighted condition. Such increase in the rate of taxation shall be accomplished through application of a factor to the millage rate applied to the property, so that such property shall be taxed at a higher millage rate than the millage rate generally applied in the county or municipality, or otherwise as may be provided by general law.

(4) The ordinance may, but shall not be required to, segregate revenues arising from any increased rate of ad valorem taxation and provide for use of such revenues only for community redevelopment purposes;

(5) The ordinance shall specify ascertainable standards for rehabilitation through remedial actions or redevelopment with which the owner of property may comply in order to have the property removed from identification as maintained in a blighted condition. As used herein, the term 'blighted condition' shall include, at a minimum, property that constitutes endangerment to public health or safety;

(6) The ordinance shall specify a decreased rate of ad valorem taxation to be applied for a specified period of time after the county or municipality has accepted a plan submitted by the owner for remedial action or redevelopment of the blighted property and the owner is in compliance with the terms of the plan. Such decrease in the rate of taxation shall be accomplished through application of a factor to the millage rate applied to the property, so that such property shall be taxed at a lower millage rate than the millage rate generally applied in the county or municipality, or otherwise as may be provided by general law.

(7) The ordinance may contain such other matters as are consistent with the intent and provisions of this subparagraph and general law. Variations in rate of taxation as authorized under this subparagraph shall be a permissible variation in the uniformity of taxation otherwise required. The increase or decrease in rate of taxation accomplished through a change in the otherwise applicable millage rate shall affect only the general millage rate for county or municipal maintenance and operations. A county and one or more municipalities in the county may, but shall not be required to, establish a joint community redevelopment tax incentive program through the adoption of concurrent ordinances. No Act of the General Assembly shall be required for counties and municipalities to establish community redevelopment tax incentive programs. However, the General Assembly may by general law regulate, restrict, or limit the powers granted to counties and municipalities under this subparagraph.

Paragraph VIII. Limitation on the taxing power and contributions of counties, municipalities, and political subdivisions

The General Assembly shall not authorize any county, municipality, or other political subdivision of this state, through taxation, contribution, or otherwise, to appropriate money for or to lend its credit to any person or to any nonpublic corporation or association except for purely charitable purposes.

Paragraph IX. Immunity of counties, municipalities, and school districts

The General Assembly may waive the immunity of counties, municipalities, and school districts by law.

SECTION III. INTERGOVERNMENTAL RELATIONS

Paragraph I. Intergovernmental contracts

(a) The state, or any institution, department, or other agency thereof, and any county, municipality, school district, or other political subdivision of the state may contract for any period not exceeding 50 years with each other or with any other public agency, public corporation, or public authority for joint services, for the provision of services, or for the joint or separate use of facilities or equipment; but such contracts must deal with activities, services, or facilities which the contracting parties are authorized by law to undertake or provide. By way of specific instance and not limitation, a mutual undertaking by a local government entity to borrow and an undertaking by the state or a state authority to lend funds from and to one another for water or sewerage facilities or systems or for regional or multijurisdictional solid waste recycling or solid waste facilities or systems pursuant to law shall be a provision for services and an activity within the meaning of this Paragraph.

(b) Subject to such limitations as may be provided by general law, any county, municipality, or political subdivision thereof may, in connection with any contracts authorized in this Paragraph, convey any existing facilities or equipment to the state or to any public agency, public corporation, or public authority.

(c) Any county, municipality, or any combination thereof, may contract with any public agency, public corporation, or public authority for the care, maintenance, and hospitalization of its indigent sick and may as a part of such contract agree to pay for the cost of acquisition, construction, modernization, or repairs of necessary land, buildings, and facilities by such public agency, public corporation, or public authority and provide for the payment of such services and the cost to such public agency, public corporation, or public authority of acquisition, construction, modernization, or repair of land, buildings, and facilities from revenues realized by such county, municipality, or any combination thereof from any taxes authorized by this Constitution or revenues derived from any other source.

Paragraph II. Local government reorganization

(a) The General Assembly may provide by law for any matters necessary or convenient to authorize the consolidation of the governmental and corporate powers and functions vested in municipalities with the governmental and corporate powers and functions vested in a county or counties in which such municipalities are located; provided, however, that no such consolidation shall become effective unless separately approved by a majority of the qualified voters of the county or each of the counties and of the municipality or each of the municipalities located within such county or counties containing at least 10 percent of the population of the county in which located voting thereon in such manner as may be prescribed in such law. Such law may provide procedures and requirements for the establishment of charter commissions to draft proposed charters for the consolidated government, and the General Assembly is expressly authorized to delegate its powers to such charter commissions for such purposes so that the governmental consolidation proposed by a charter commission may become effective without the necessity of further action by the General Assembly; or such law may require that the recommendation of any such charter commission be implemented by a subsequent local law.

(b) The General Assembly may provide by general law for alternatives other than governmental consolidation as authorized in subparagraph (a) above for the reorganization of county and municipal governments, including, but not limited to, procedures to establish a single governing body as the governing authority of a county and a municipality or municipalities located within such county or for the redistribution of powers between a county and a municipality or municipalities located within the county. Such law may require the form of governmental reorganization authorized by such law to be approved by the qualified voters directly affected thereby voting in such manner as may be required in such law.

(c) Nothing in this Paragraph shall be construed to limit the authority of the General Assembly to repeal municipal charters without a referendum.

SECTION IV. TAXATION POWER OF COUNTY AND MUNICIPAL GOVERNMENTS

Paragraph I. Power of taxation

(a) Except as otherwise provided in this Paragraph, the governing authority of any county, municipality, or combination thereof may exercise the power of taxation as authorized by this Constitution or by general law.

(b) In the absence of a general law:

(1) County governing authorities may be authorized by local law to levy and collect business and occupational license taxes and license fees only in the unincorporated areas of the counties. The General Assembly may provide that the revenues raised by such tax or fee be spent for the provision of services only in the unincorporated areas of the county.

(2) Municipal governing authorities may be authorized by local law to levy and collect taxes and fees in the corporate limits of the municipalities.

(c) The General Assembly may provide by law for the taxation of insurance companies on the basis of gross direct premiums received from insurance policies within the unincorporated areas of counties. The tax authorized herein may be imposed by the state or by counties or by the state for county purposes as may be provided by law. The General Assembly may further provide by law for the reduction, only upon taxable property within the unincorporated areas of counties, of the ad valorem tax millage rate for county or county school district purposes or for the reduction of such ad valorem tax millage rate for both such purposes in connection with imposing or authorizing the imposition of the tax authorized herein or in connection with providing for the distribution of the proceeds derived from the tax authorized herein.

Paragraph II. Power of expenditure
The governing authority of any county, municipality, or combination thereof may expend public funds to perform any public service or public function as authorized by this Constitution or by law or to perform any other service or function as authorized by this Constitution or by general law.
Paragraph III. Purposes of taxation; allocation of taxes. No levy need state the particular purposes for which the same was made nor shall any taxes collected be allocated for any particular purpose, unless otherwise provided by this Constitution or by law.

Paragraph IV. Tax allocation; regional facilities
As used in this Paragraph, the term 'regional facilities' means industrial parks, business parks, conference centers, convention centers, airports, athletic facilities, recreation facilities, jails or correctional facilities, or other similar or related economic development parks, centers, or facilities or any combination thereof. Notwithstanding any other provision of this Constitution,

a county or municipality is authorized to enter into contracts with:

(1) any county which is contiguous to such county or the county in which such municipality is located;
(2) any municipality located in such a contiguous county or the same county; or
(3) any combination thereof. Any such contract may be for the purpose of allocating the proceeds of ad valorem taxes assessed and collected on real property located in such county or municipality with such other counties or municipalities with which the assessing county or municipality has entered into agreements for the development of one or more regional facilities and the allocation of other revenues generated from such regional facilities. Any such regional facility may be publicly or privately initiated. The allocation of such tax proceeds and other revenues shall be determined by contract between the affected local governments. Such contract shall provide for the manner of development, operation, and management of the regional facility and the sharing of expenses among the contracting local governments and shall specify the percentage of ad valorem taxes and other revenues to be allocated and the method of allocation to each contracting local government. Unless otherwise provided by law, such a regional facility will qualify for the greatest dollar amount of income tax credits which may be provided for by general law for any of the counties or municipalities which have entered into an agreement for the development of the regional facility, regardless of the county or municipality in which the business is physically located. The authority granted to counties and municipalities under this Paragraph shall be subject to any conditions, limitations, and restrictions which may be imposed by general law.

SECTION V. LIMITATION ON LOCAL DEBT

Paragraph I. Debt limitations of counties, municipalities, and other political subdivisions

(a) The debt incurred by any county, municipality, or other political subdivision of this state, including debt incurred on behalf of any special district, shall never exceed 10 percent of the assessed value of all taxable property within such county, municipality, or political subdivision; and no such county, municipality, or other political subdivision shall incur any new debt without the assent of a majority of the qualified voters of such county, municipality, or political subdivision voting in an election held for that purpose as provided by law.
(b) Notwithstanding subparagraph (a) of this Paragraph, all local school systems which are authorized by law on June 30, 1983, to incur debt in excess of 10 percent of the assessed value of all taxable property therein shall continue to be authorized to incur such debt.

Paragraph II. Special district debt

Any county, municipality, or political subdivision of this state may incur debt on behalf of any special district created pursuant to Paragraph VI of Section II of this article. Such debt may be incurred on behalf of such special district where the county, municipality, or other political subdivision shall have, at or before the time of incurring such debt, provided for the assessment and collection of an annual tax within the special district sufficient in amount to pay the principal of and interest on such debt within 30 years from the incurrence thereof; and no such county, municipality, or other political subdivision shall incur any debt on behalf of such special district without the assent of a majority of the qualified voters of such special district voting in an election held for that purpose as provided by law. No such county, municipality, or other political subdivision shall incur any debt on behalf of such special district in an amount which, when taken together with all other debt outstanding incurred by such county, municipality, or political subdivision and on behalf of any such special district, exceeds 10 percent of the assessed value of all taxable property within such county, municipality, or political subdivision. The proceeds of the tax collected as provided herein shall be placed in a sinking fund to be held on behalf of such special district and used exclusively to pay off the principal of and interest on such debt thereafter maturing. Such moneys shall be held and kept separate and apart from all other revenues collected and may be invested and reinvested as provided by law.

Paragraph III. Refunding of outstanding indebtedness.
The governing authority of any county, municipality, or other political subdivision of this state may provide for the refunding of outstanding bonded indebtedness without the necessity of a referendum being held therefor, provided that neither the term of the original debt is extended nor the interest rate of the original debt is increased. The principal amount of any debt issued in connection with such refunding may exceed the principal amount being refunded in order to reduce the total principal and interest payment requirements over the remaining term of the original issue. The proceeds of the refunding issue shall be used solely to retire the original debt. The original debt refunded shall not constitute debt within the meaning of Paragraph I of this section; but the refunding issue shall constitute a debt such as will count against the limitation on debt measured by 10 percent of assessed value of taxable property as expressed in Paragraph I of this section.

Paragraph IV. Exceptions to debt limitations
Notwithstanding the debt limitations provided in Paragraph I of this section and without the necessity for a referendum being held therefor, the governing authority of any county, municipality, or other political subdivision of this state may, subject to the conditions and limitations as may be provided by general law:

(1) Accept and use funds granted by and obtain loans from the federal government or any agency thereof pursuant to conditions imposed by federal law.

(2) Incur debt, by way of borrowing from any person, corporation, or association as well as from the state, to pay in whole or in part the cost of property valuation and equalization programs for ad valorem tax purposes.

Paragraph V. Temporary loans authorized

The governing authority of any county, municipality, or other political subdivision of this state may incur debt by obtaining temporary loans in each year to pay expenses. The aggregate amount of all such loans shall not exceed 75 percent of the total gross income from taxes collected in the last preceding year. Such loans shall be payable on or before December 31 of the calendar year in which such loan is made. No such loan may be obtained when there is a loan then unpaid obtained in any prior year. No such county, municipality, or other political subdivision of this state shall incur in any one calendar year an aggregate of such temporary loans or other contracts, notes, warrants, or obligations for current expenses in excess of the total anticipated revenue for such calendar year.

Paragraph VI. Levy of taxes to pay bonds; sinking fund required

Any county, municipality, or other political subdivision of this state shall at or before the time of incurring bonded indebtedness provide for the assessment and collection of an annual tax sufficient in amount to pay the principal and interest of said debt within 30 years from the incurring of such bonded indebtedness. The proceeds of this tax, together with any other moneys collected for this purpose, shall be placed in a sinking fund to be used exclusively for paying the principal of and interest on such bonded debt. Such moneys shall be held and kept separate and apart from all other revenues collected and may be invested and reinvested as provided by law. -67 Paragraph VII. Validity of prior bond issues. Any and all bond issues validated and issued prior to June 30, 1983, shall continue to be valid.

SECTION VI. REVENUE BONDS

Paragraph I. Revenue bonds; general limitations
Any county, municipality, or other political subdivision of this state may issue revenue bonds as provided by general law. The obligation represented by revenue bonds shall be repayable only out of the revenue derived from the project and shall not be deemed to be a debt of the issuing political subdivision. No such issuing political subdivision shall exercise the power of taxation for the purpose of paying any part of the principal or interest of any such revenue bonds.

Paragraph II. Revenue bonds; special limitations
Where revenue bonds are issued by any county, municipality, or other political subdivision of this state in order to buy, construct, extend, operate, or maintain gas or electric generating or distribution systems and necessary appurtenances thereof and the gas or electric generating or distribution system extends beyond the limits of the county in which the municipality or other political subdivision is located, then its services rendered and property located outside said county shall be subject to taxation and regulation in the same manner as are privately owned and operated utilities.

Paragraph III. Development authorities
The development of trade, commerce, industry, and employment opportunities being a public purpose vital to the welfare of the people of this state, the General Assembly may create development authorities to promote and further such purposes or may authorize the creation of such an authority by any county or municipality or combination thereof under such uniform terms and conditions as it may deem necessary. The General Assembly may exempt from taxation development authority obligations, properties, activities, or income and may authorize the issuance of revenue bonds by such authorities which shall not constitute an indebtedness of the state within the meaning of Section V of this article.

Paragraph IV. Validation
The General Assembly shall provide for the validation of any revenue bonds authorized and shall provide that such validation shall thereafter be incontestable and conclusive.

Paragraph V. Validity of prior revenue bond issues
All revenue bonds issued and validated prior to June 30, 1983, shall continue to be valid.

SECTION VII. COMMUNITY IMPROVEMENT DISTRICTS

Paragraph I. Creation
The General Assembly may by local law create one or more community improvement districts for any county or municipality or provide for the creation of one or more community improvement districts by any county or municipality.

Paragraph II. Purposes
The purpose of a community improvement district shall be the provision of any one or more of the following governmental services and facilities:

(1) Street and road construction and maintenance, including curbs, sidewalks, street lights, and devices to control the flow of traffic on streets and roads.
(2) Parks and recreational areas and facilities.
(3) Storm water and sewage collection and disposal systems.
(4) Development, storage, treatment, purification, and distribution of water.
(5) Public transportation.
(6) Terminal and dock facilities and parking facilities.
(7) Such other services and facilities as may be provided for by general law.

Paragraph III. Administration

(a) Any law creating or providing for the creation of a community improvement district shall designate the governing authority of the municipality or county for which the community improvement district is created as the administrative body or otherwise shall provide for the establishment and membership of an administrative body for the community improvement district. Any such law creating or providing for the creation of an administrative body for the community improvement district other than the municipal or county governing authority shall provide for representation of the governing authority of each county and municipality within which the community improvement district is wholly or partially located on the administrative body of the community improvement district.
(b) Any law creating or providing for the creation of a community improvement district shall provide that the creation of the community improvement district shall be conditioned upon:

(1) The adoption of a resolution consenting to the creation of the community improvement district by:

(A) The governing authority of the county if the community improvement district is located wholly within the unincorporated area of a county;
(B) The governing authority of the municipality if the community improvement district is located wholly within the incorporated area of a municipality; or
(C) The governing authorities of the county and the municipality if the community improvement district is located partially within the unincorporated area of a county and partially within the incorporated area of a municipality; and

(2) Written consent to the creation of the community improvement district by:

(A) A majority of the owners of real property within the community improvement district which will be subject to taxes, fees, and assessments levied by the administrative body of the community improvement district; and
(B) The owners of real property within the community improvement district which constitutes at least 75 percent by value of all real property within the community improvement district which will be subject to taxes, fees, and assessments levied by the administrative body of the community improvement district; and for this purpose value shall be determined by the most recent approved county ad valorem tax digest.
(c) The administrative body of each community improvement district may be authorized to levy taxes, fees, and assessments within the community improvement district only on real property used nonresidentially, specifically excluding all property used for residential, agricultural, or forestry purposes and specifically excluding tangible personal property and intangible property. Any tax, fee, or assessment so levied shall not exceed 2 1/2 percent of the assessed value of the real property or such lower limit as may be established by law. The law creating or providing for the creation of a community improvement district shall provide that taxes, fees, and assessments levied by the administrative body of the community improvement district shall be equitably apportioned among the properties subject to such taxes, fees, and assessments according to the need for governmental services and facilities created by the degree of density of development of each such property. The law creating or providing for the creation of a community improvement district shall provide that the proceeds of taxes, fees, and assessments levied by the administrative body of the community improvement district shall be used only for the purpose of providing governmental services and facilities which are specially required by the degree of density of development within the community improvement district and not for the purpose of providing those governmental services and facilities provided to the county or municipality as a whole. Any tax, fee, or assessment so levied shall be collected by the county or municipality for which the community improvement district is created in the same manner

as taxes, fees, and assessments levied by such county or municipality. The proceeds of taxes, fees, and assessments so levied, less such fee to cover the costs of collection as may be specified by law, shall be transmitted by the collecting county or municipality to the administrative body of the community improvement district and shall be expended by the administrative body of the community improvement district only for the purposes authorized by this Section.

Paragraph IV. Debt
The administrative body of a community improvement district may incur debt, as authorized by law, without regard to the requirements of Section V of this Article, which debt shall be backed by the full faith, credit, and taxing power of the community improvement district but shall not be an obligation of the State of Georgia or any other unit of government of the State of Georgia other than the community improvement district.
Paragraph V. Cooperation with local governments. The services and facilities provided pursuant to this Section shall be provided for in a cooperation agreement executed jointly by the administrative body and the governing authority of the county or municipality for which the community improvement district is created. The provisions of this section shall in no way limit the authority of any county or municipality to provide services or facilities within any community improvement district; and any county or municipality shall retain full and complete authority and control over any of its facilities located within a community improvement district. Said control shall include but not be limited to the modification of, access to, and degree and type of services provided through or by facilities of the municipality or county. Nothing contained in this Section shall be construed to limit or preempt the application of any governmental laws, ordinances, resolutions, or regulations to any community improvement district or the services or facilities provided therein.
Paragraph VI. Regulation by general law. The General Assembly by general law may regulate, restrict, and limit the creation of community improvement districts and the exercise of the powers of administrative bodies of community improvement districts.

ARTICLE X: AMENDMENTS TO THE CONSTITUTION

SECTION I. CONSTITUTION, HOW AMENDED

Paragraph I. Proposals to amend the Constitution; new Constitution

Amendments to this Constitution or a new Constitution may be proposed by the General Assembly or by a constitutional convention, as provided in this article. Only amendments which are of general and uniform applicability throughout the state shall be proposed, passed, or submitted to the people.

Paragraph II. Proposals by the General Assembly; submission to the people

A proposal by the General Assembly to amend this Constitution or to provide for a new Constitution shall originate as a resolution in either the Senate or the House of Representatives and, if approved by two-thirds of the members to which each house is entitled in a roll-call vote entered on their respective journals, shall be submitted to the electors of the entire state at the next general election which is held in the even-numbered years. A summary of such proposal shall be prepared by the Attorney General, the Legislative Counsel, and the Secretary of State and shall be published in the official organ of each county and, if deemed advisable by the 'Constitutional Amendments Publication Board,' in not more than 20 other newspapers in the state designated by such board which meet the qualifications for being selected as the official organ of a county. Said board shall be composed of the Governor, the Lieutenant Governor, and the Speaker of the House of Representatives. Such summary shall be published once each week for three consecutive weeks immediately preceding the day of the general election at which such proposal is to be submitted. The language to be used in submitting a proposed amendment or a new Constitution shall be in such words as the General Assembly may provide in the resolution or, in the absence thereof, in such language as the Governor may prescribe. A copy of the entire proposed amendment or of a new Constitution shall be filed in the office of the judge of the probate court of each county and shall be available for public inspection; and the summary of the proposal shall so indicate. The General Assembly is hereby authorized to provide by law for additional matters relative to the publication and distribution of proposed amendments and summaries not in conflict with the provisions of this Paragraph. If such proposal is ratified by a majority of the electors qualified to vote for members of the General Assembly voting thereon in such general election, such proposal shall become a part of this Constitution or shall become a new Constitution, as the case may be. Any proposal so approved shall take effect as provided in Paragraph VI of this article. When more than one amendment is submitted at the same time, they shall be so submitted as to enable the electors to vote on each amendment separately, provided that one or more new articles or related changes in one or more articles may be submitted as a single amendment.

Paragraph III. Repeal or amendment of proposal
Any proposal by the General Assembly to amend this Constitution or for a new Constitution may be amended or repealed by the same General Assembly which adopted such proposal by the affirmative vote of two-thirds of the members to which each house is entitled in a roll-call vote entered on their respective journals, if such action is taken at least two months prior to the date of the election at which such proposal is to be submitted to the people.

Paragraph IV. Constitutional convention; how called
No convention of the people shall be called by the General Assembly to amend this Constitution or to propose a new Constitution, unless by the concurrence of two-thirds of the members to which each house of the General Assembly is entitled. The representation in said convention shall be based on population as near as practicable. A proposal by the convention to amend this Constitution or for a new Constitution shall be advertised, submitted to, and ratified by the people in the same manner provided for advertisement, submission, and ratification of proposals to amend the Constitution by the General Assembly.

The General Assembly is hereby authorized to provide the procedure by which a convention is to be called and under which such convention shall operate and for other matters relative to such constitutional convention.

Paragraph V. Veto not permitted
The Governor shall not have the right to veto any proposal by the General Assembly or by a convention to amend this Constitution or to provide a new Constitution.

Paragraph VI. Effective date of amendments or of a new Constitution
Unless the amendment or the new Constitution itself or the resolution proposing the amendment or the new Constitution shall provide otherwise, an amendment to this Constitution or a new Constitution shall become effective on the first day of January following its ratification.

ARTICLE XI: MISCELLANEOUS PROVISIONS

SECTION I. MISCELLANEOUS PROVISIONS

Paragraph I. Continuation of officers, boards, commissions, and authorities

(a) Except as otherwise provided in this Constitution, the officers of the state and all political subdivisions thereof in office on June 30, 1983, shall continue in the exercise of their functions and duties, subject to the provisions of laws applicable thereto and subject to the provisions of this Constitution.
(b) All boards, commissions, and authorities specifically named in the Constitution of 1976 which are not specifically named in this Constitution shall remain as statutory boards, commissions, and authorities; and all constitutional and statutory provisions relating thereto in force and effect on June 30, 1983, shall remain in force and effect as statutory law unless and until changed by the General Assembly.

Paragraph II. Preservation of existing laws; judicial review
All laws in force and effect on June 30, 1983, not inconsistent with this Constitution shall remain in force and effect; but such laws may be amended or repealed and shall be subject to judicial decision as to their validity when passed and to any limitations imposed by their own terms.

Paragraph III. Proceedings of courts and administrative tribunals confirmed
All judgments, decrees, orders, and other proceedings of the several courts and administrative tribunals of this state, heretofore made within the limits of their several jurisdictions, are hereby ratified and affirmed, subject only to reversal or modification in the manner provided by law.

Paragraph IV. Continuation of certain constitutional amendments for a period of four years

(a) The following amendments to the Constitutions of 1877, 1945, and 1976 shall continue in force and effect as part of this Constitution until July 1, 1987, at which time said amendments shall be repealed and shall be deleted as a part of this Constitution unless any such amendment shall be specifically continued in force and effect without amendment either by a local law enacted prior to July 1, 1987, with or without a referendum as provided by law, or by an ordinance or resolution duly adopted prior to July 1, 1987, by the local governing authority in the manner provided for the adoption of home rule amendments to its charter or local act:

(1) amendments to the Constitution of 1877 and the Constitution of 1945 which were continued in force and effect as a part of the Constitution of 1976 pursuant to the provisions of Article XIII, Section I, Paragraph II of the Constitution of 1976 which are in force and effect on the effective date of this Constitution;
(2) amendments to the Constitution of 1976 which were ratified as general amendments but which by their terms applied principally to a particular political subdivision or subdivisions which are in force and effect on the effective date of this Constitution;
(3) amendments to the Constitution of 1976 which were ratified not as general amendments which are in force and effect on the effective date of this Constitution; and
(4) amendments to the Constitution of 1976 of the type provided for in the immediately preceding two subparagraphs (2) and (3) of this Paragraph which were ratified at the same time this Constitution was ratified.

(b) Any amendment which is continued in force and effect after July 1, 1987, pursuant to the provisions of subparagraph (a) of this Paragraph shall be continued in force and effect as a part of this Constitution, except that such amendment may thereafter be repealed but may not be amended. The repeal of any such amendment shall be accomplished by local Act of the General Assembly, the effectiveness of which shall be conditioned on its approval by a majority of the qualified voters voting thereon in each of the particular political subdivisions affected by the amendment.

(c) All laws enacted pursuant to those amendments to the Constitution which are not continued in force and effect pursuant to subparagraph (a) of this Paragraph shall be repealed on July 1, 1987. All laws validly enacted on, before, or after July 1, 1987, and pursuant to the specific authorization of an amendment continued in force and effect pursuant to the provisions of subparagraph (a) of this Paragraph shall be legal, valid, and constitutional under this Constitution. Nothing in this subparagraph (c) shall be construed to revive any law not in force and effect on June 30, 1987.

(d) Notwithstanding the provisions of subparagraphs (a) and (b), the following amendments to the Constitutions of 1877 and 1945 shall be continued in force as a part of this Constitution: amendments to the Constitution of 1877 and the Constitution of 1945 which created or authorized the creation of metropolitan rapid transit authorities, port authorities, and industrial areas and which were continued in force as a part of the Constitution of 1976 pursuant to the provisions of Article XIII, Section I, Paragraph II of the Constitution of 1976 and which are in force on the effective date of this Constitution.

(e) Any person owning property in an industrial area described in subparagraph (d) of this Paragraph may voluntarily remove the property from the industrial area by filing a certificate to that effect with the clerk of the superior court for the county in which the property is located. Once the certificate is filed, the property described in the certificate, together with all public streets and public rights of way within the property, abutting the property, or connecting the property to property outside the industrial area, shall no longer be in the industrial area and shall upon the filing of the certificate be annexed to the city which provides water service to the property, or if no city provides water service shall be annexed to the city providing fire service as provided under the constitutional amendments that created such industrial areas described in subparagraph (d) of this Paragraph. The filing of a certificate shall be irrevocable and shall bind the owners, their heirs, and their assigns. The term 'owner' includes anyone with a legal or equitable ownership in property but does not include a beneficiary of any trust or a partner in any partnership owning an interest in the property or anyone owning an easement right in the property.

Paragraph V. Special commission created
Amendments to the Constitution of 1976 which were determined to be general and which were submitted to and ratified by the people of the entire state at the same time this Constitution was ratified shall be incorporated and made a part of this Constitution as provided in this Paragraph. There is hereby created a commission to be composed of the Governor, the President of the Senate, the Speaker of the House of Representatives, the Attorney General, and the Legislative Counsel, which is hereby authorized and directed to incorporate such amendments into this Constitution at the places deemed most appropriate to the commission. The commission shall make only such changes in the language of this Constitution and of such amendments as are necessary to incorporate properly such amendments into this Constitution and shall complete its duties prior to July 1, 1983. The commission shall deliver to the Secretary of State this Constitution with those amendments incorporated therein, and such document shall be the Constitution of the State of Georgia. In order that the commission may perform its duties, this Paragraph shall become effective as soon as it has been officially determined that this Constitution has been ratified. The commission shall stand abolished upon the completion of its duties.

Paragraph VI. Effective date
Except as provided in Paragraph V of this section, this Constitution shall become effective on July 1, 1983; and, except as otherwise provided in this Constitution, all previous Constitutions and all amendments thereto shall thereupon stand repealed.

www.ingramcontent.com/pod-product-compliance
Lightning Source LLC
Chambersburg PA
CBHW052257220526
45471CB00001B/381